Honey, I Dunked the Kids shoul
Wrote a Bestseller! Phil Callawa
as a Christian husband and fath
laughs along the way. I enjoyed every page! You will too!

—**Martha Bolton**
Author and Bob Hope staff writer

Need a shot of sunlight on a cloudy day? This book's for you. Need a whisper of His love in a noisy life? You'll hear it as you turn these pages. Need a touch of calm in the midst of chaos? Phil Callaway has provided it in *Honey, I Dunked the Kids*. This book is for all who desire to love God and love life and get confused doing both.

—**Max Lucado**
Author of *Eye of the Storm,*
The Applause of Heaven,
Six Hours One Friday

From the moment I picked the book up to the moment I put it down my entire body convulsed with laughter and tears streamed down my cheeks. Someday I shall read it. . . . Seriously, folks, *Honey, I Dunked the Kids* is an excellent read. Phil Callaway does a great job of taking everyday experiences, putting a humorous spin to them, and making the reader think. If you enjoy humor that causes you to consider longer than cackle, you'll enjoy Phil's book.

—**Joel A. Freeman**
Author of *God Is Not Fair*
and chaplain of the NBA
Washington Bullets

Keep a copy of this book handy for those times when your three-year-old decides to give the dog a haircut or your baby spits strained squash on your new suit. With insightful wit, Phil Callaway reminds us of the extraordinary wonder of parenthood, on even the most ordinary of days.

—**Ellen Santilli Vaughn**
V.P. of Executive Communications,
Prison Fellowship
Co-author of *Loving God, The Body,*
Against the Night

For the last few years I have enjoyed reading Phil Callaway's articles in *Servant* magazine. His transparent communication penetrates the heart and gives a lift, a laugh, and a lesson. *Honey, I Dunked the Kids* is a great companion for all who participate in this adventure called *family*.

—**Steve Green**
Christian recording artist

I rarely enjoy a book as much as I did *Honey, I Dunked the Kids*. Very few people can make me laugh or cry. But as I read Phil's book, I did both, to the bewilderment of the airline passengers seated around me. You won't want to put this book down, but do it anyway. After all, a gourmet meal is better savored slowly.

—**Ken Davis**
Author of *Dynamic Communication*,
I Don't Remember Dropping the Skunk,
I Just Remember Trying to Breathe,
How to Live With Your Kids
When You've Already Lost Your Mind

Our lives are parables through which God chooses to speak. Phil Callaway's new book makes the business of listening to your life more than just bearable, but truly joyful. God speaks through the small and ordinary in extraordinary ways. Phil has listened and heard—and thankfully decided to share it with us.

—**Michael Card**
Author, teacher and singer/songwriter

This book could be called *I used to Be a Perfect Parent—Until I Had Kids!* It is so refreshing to read a book by a real parent with real kids. This is my kind of book—easy to read, down-home humor, and illustrations that mirror family life in today's home. Phil will lovingly challenge you to be the parent you really want to be. *Honey, I Dunked the Kids* is a must read for every parent, and I don't say that lightly.

—**Al Menconi**
Speaker, author

Honey, I Dunked the Kids

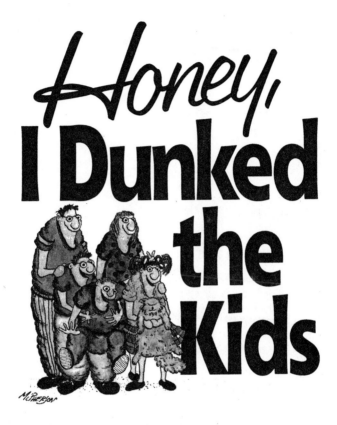

Phil Callaway

HARVEST HOUSE PUBLISHERS
EUGENE, OREGON 97402

Except where otherwise indicated, all Scripture quotations in this book are taken from the Holy Bible, New International Version®, Copyright © 1973, 1978, 1984 by the International Bible Society. Used by permission of Zondervan Publishing House. The "NIV" and "New International Version" trademarks are registered in the United States Patent and Trademark Office by International Bible Society.

Some of the stories in *Honey, I Dunked the Kids* have appeared in a different form in *Servant* magazine, a ministry of Prairie Bible Institute, Three Hills, Alberta, Canada.

HONEY, I DUNKED THE KIDS

Copyright © 1993 by Harvest House Publishers
Illustration Copyright © by John McPherson
Published by Harvest House Publishers
Eugene, Oregon 97402

Library of Congress Cataloging-in-Publication Data

Callaway, Phil, 1961-
     Honey, I dunked the kids / Phil Callaway.
         p.   cm.
     ISBN 1-56507-061-5
     1. Family—Religious life.   2. Family—United States—Humor.
  3. Family—United States—Anecdotes.   4. Parenting—Religious
  aspects—Christianity.   I. Title.
  BV4526.2.C24   1993
  248.4—dc20   93-18873
                                                                  CIP

93 94 95 96 97 98 99 00 — 12 11 10 9 8 7 6 5 4 3

Dedication

For 31 years of your love.
For 50 years of faithfulness.
For saying I could when I thought I couldn't.
For saying I couldn't when I desperately wanted to.
For late-night talks and early-morning lullabies.
And, most of all, for mirroring Him.
For you, Mom and Dad.

Contents

Thanks

My wife, Ramona: You have been my faithful friend for 15 years. You have critiqued when others criticized. You have examined these pages for historical accuracy (and reminded me that I don't need to lie—the truth is entertaining enough). You have always pointed me higher, and I can think of more than three tax-deductible reasons why I couldn't have written this book without you.

Stephen, Rachael, and Jeffrey: When I am older, balder, dentured, and forgetful, I pray that you'll remember these three things: my love for God, my love for Mom, and my love for you.

Servant magazine readers: Your kind letters (and letters of the other kind) have spurred me on through the early-morning hours. I wouldn't have done this without you.

The staff at Prairie Bible Institute: The opportunity to work beside you has been a thrill, as has been your encouragement. I can't imagine working at a better school, with better people.

Eileen Mason: for that first phone call from Harvest House.

My new friends at Harvest House: for believing, for patience, for keeping Him the bottom line.

My Savior, Jesus Christ: for captivating me from early childhood... with a story.

Off the Top

Since I began writing stories on family life for *Servant* magazine, I have received letters from 8-year-olds and 92-year-olds alike. From places like Moose Jaw and Irian Jaya. Perhaps what interested me more than their addresses was the common thread in their letters. "Phil," they wrote one after another, "not since Solomon sat down to that very first Macintosh has the world been blessed with such wisdom." Just kidding there. Actually, what they said was simply this: I have seen my family reflected in yours.

Of course they all put it in different ways. One dear lady told me confidentially (and that's why I would never reprint it, especially in a book) that "throughout almost 50 years of marriage I have wondered if other couples struggle like we have to make their relationship work. I'm encouraged to know that you have too." A young mother wrote, "Most of the Christian couples I know seem to either have all the answers or none of the answers when it comes to raising their families. Thanks for your honesty and for addressing the important questions."

On the other hand, a gentleman in Ohio wrote to inform me that "anyone who talks about his own faults like you do obviously has a low self-image."

So in defense of what little self-esteem I may have left after reading his letter, allow me to explain that when I sat down to write these stories, I did so realizing the truth of the following four-point outline:

1. There are many wonderful books covering child-rearing techniques.
2. I am neither qualified nor capable of writing one.
3. By the time I am a qualified father, I will either be deceased or, at the very least, unemployed.
4. I will not be bitter about the first three points.

What you will find on these pages is not the final word on relationships or the advice of a father who has it all together and remembers where he put it, but some entertaining and true stories that took place during the four most interesting years of my life. And, more than anything, I hope these tales will point you beyond our family to the One who delights in turning adults into children, teachers into learners, tax-collectors into civil servants, and houses into homes: Jesus Christ.

So whether you're in Moose Jaw, Irian Jaya, or New York, these stories are for you. May you find your family here. And should you have half as much fun reading this as I have had writing it, then I think we shall both be happy.

—Phil Callaway
Three Hills, Alberta, Canada

1
Shotgun Memories

"DAD, THE NINTENDO ISN'T TURNED ON. THAT'S 'ROSEANNE' YOU'RE WATCHING."

" —————————————————————————

Regret for the things we did can be tempered by time; it is regret for the things we did not do that is inconsolable.

—Sydney J. Harris

Now is the watchword of the wise.

—Charles Haddon
Spurgeon

————————————————————— **"**

I awoke and lay still in the darkness. From my bed I could hear the ticktock of the living room clock. The enticing aroma of breakfast wound its way down the hall. It was early, but suddenly I was wide awake.

Morning was finally here. The morning of the hunt.

As we drove down the dusty gravel road that cold November day, I knew this would be no ordinary hunting trip. I had been hunting before, but today something was different. Today I was with Dad.

Alone.

Behind us lay the 12-gauge shotgun, brought out on special occasions such as this. In front of us lay what would become one of the most vivid memories of my life.

Being the youngest of five, it was a rare occasion when I could be alone with Dad. He worked hard six days a week and was gone many weekends. But today he was all mine. Today I was with the greatest hunter in the world. My real-live hero. Someone who had not only tracked, but also shot, skinned, fried, and eaten an entire rabbit.

Driving along I listened as he recounted in vivid detail pre-vious hunting adventures. This was where he had shot a pheas-ant. On the other side of that thicket was an ideal pond for ducks. Rabbits were everywhere if you turned down this road.

Outside, the cold prairie wind brought broad, fluffy snowflakes to rest on the frozen ground, and the last few leaves struggled to release themselves from the grip of the tall poplar trees. But inside our car the sun was shining.

We entered the forest in single file. I was careful not to step on any branches. He was careful not to get too far ahead. Adventure seemed to lurk behind every bush. "Sshhh," he would say, lifting his finger to his lips. "You never know...." And I was deathly quiet.

Standing in the cold, we ate our lunch of sandwiches. "Stomp your feet like this," Dad would say.

"But won't it scare the rabbits away?"

He smiled in response. "It will keep you warm. Besides, I haven't even seen a rabbit track."

"I'm cold," I said.

"Should we go home?"

"Sure."

Soon we were on our way. And although we didn't have a trophy to show for our trip, I didn't mind.

I had been with the hunter.

———

Years later, we were alone again as we drove down those same dusty roads. The shotgun was in the backseat, but this time it would serve a different purpose.

For weeks we had watched the paper for just the right car. Something old. And something cheap. We had finally found it in the form of a 1970 Ford Maverick, and now we hoped to claim the prize.

Arriving at the farmhouse, we carefully examined what was to become my first vehicle. And when it came time to pay up, Dad took out his precious shotgun and traded it in.

———

As I sat up late watching these memories swirl through my mind, I wondered what it was that had made those times with Dad so special. Was it the thrill of the hunt? Or of buying my first car? No. The hunting trip wasn't very successful and, believe me, the car didn't last forever. But the memories would, because someone who had a to-do list as long as my arm had taken the time to be alone with me. The love of an imperfect Dad had mirrored the perfect love of my heavenly Father.

I thought of my own children, and of the times my son had tried to get my attention while I read the paper or watched a hockey game. I thought of evenings at work. I had deadlines to meet. I was busy with important things, wasn't I? Yes, I was. But that night alone in the dark I wondered just how important these things were. I wondered if anything in the world was more significant than the children God had given me.

Quietly I got out of bed and crept down the hallway to watch my three-year-old sleep. His face was tranquil, trusting, his arm clutched tightly around his brown-and-white teddy bear. What would he remember me for? My devotion to my job? My love of books? Would he have trouble believing that God had time for him because I seldom did? Tears came to my eyes.

"Lord, help me take the time. Time to hold his hand. Time to walk with him. Time to talk with him. Time to listen. Give me the presence of mind to put the paper down. To switch off the game. To leave my work at the office. To teach him about my loving heavenly Father. To somehow make it easier for him to know that You love him because of the way I do. To show him that the most important things in life cannot be purchased; they are gifts from You."

———

After devising a way to attach little microphones to toddlers' T-shirts, researchers recently began listening in on the conversations that went on in homes. They were shocked to discover that fathers spent an average of 37 seconds per day playing and talking with their children. Their direct interaction was limited to 2.7 encounters daily, lasting 10 to 15 seconds each.

At the same time other surveys show that the average North American child will have watched 5,000 hours of TV by the time he enters first grade and 19,000 hours by the end of high school (that's over three years of watching when you count every waking hour).

It's time we wake up, dads! I have yet to meet a father who came to the end of his life wishing he had spent more time with his desk. Or his newspaper. Or his television. But I have met too many who seem to be spending the last half of their life regretting the first half.

Our children will be influenced. Our children will learn values. But it's up to us to determine from whom they learn these values. Will it be Dad or Batman? Will it be Mom or Prime Time? Let's make some memories. And let's start today. Tomorrow will be too late. You may want to begin with a simple hug, an evening at home, or a trip to the country. You may even want to throw in a shotgun.

————

Kids spell love t-i-m-e.

2
The Bare Witness

"WHATEVER YOU DO, DON'T TELL MOM HE'S IN HERE."

"

Father, each of your sermons is better than the next.
> —Young churchgoer

I learned the way a monkey learns—by watching its parents.
> —Queen Elizabeth II

Let us endeavor to so live that when we come to die, even the undertaker will be sorry.
> —Mark Twain

Example is the school of mankind.
> —Edmund Burke

Preach the Gospel all the time; if necessary use words.
> —Francis of Assissi

"

It's bath night. Around the world hurried and harried parents seize precious moments to rest and recharge while their children set uncontested Olympic records in the dunking and I-got-more-water-on-the-walls-and-ceiling-than-you-did events.

At our peculiar house, on this particular night, a four-year-old and his younger brother are all wet. The older is constructing a bubble-bath Santa beard on the younger. I can't help overhearing their conversation.

"Did you know that you've done bad things?"

"Ya." It is one of three words one-year-old Jeffrey knows. The other two are "Yep" and "Uh huh."

"You have done sins," continues the four-year-old kindly.

"Yep."

"And you shall go to hell."

"Yep."

"Hell is hot."

The one-year-old is making a hole in the soap bar.

"But you can go to heaven. Do you want to go to heaven?"

Jeffrey sips some bathwater before responding: "Uh huh."

"Then ask Jesus into your heart."

"Ya."

"I'll pray for you, okay?"

"Yep...."

Moments later an excited four-year-old stands before his parents dripping wet, wearing only a smile. "Daddy, Mommy, guess what?"

"What, Stephen?"

"Jeffrey asked Jesus into his heart."

———————

"Rachael!" A few days have passed since Stephen claimed his first trophy. He is on a roll, you might say, and he isn't about to stop now, especially at mealtime. "Did you know that you've done bad things?"

"No." It is two-year-old Rachael's most common response.

"You have done sins," the four-year-old continues, undaunted.

"Haven't." Rachael is trying to stab a pea with a fork.

"Yes, you have."

"No. Haven't."

"Yes!"

"No!"

"*Yeeeeeesss you have!*" The witnesser throws part of a sesame-seed bun at the witnessee. The bun misses. Smiles cupped behind hands quickly fade from parents' faces.

"Alright, Stephen. Come with me."

Down the hall we go, hand in hand. He is unsure of the consequences. I can't think of a thing to say. "Don't throw things at your sister" is all that comes to mind.

"Okay."

I kneel down and hold him tight. He wiggles free and we go back to sweep up the sesame seeds.

———————

Evening has come. The children are tucked in. Mom is out with my VISA card and I am in bed reading. A little pajama-clad figure with bare feet slowly pokes his head around the corner. "Hi," he says.

"Stephen, you should be asleep." My tone is unconvincing. He knows his father is a softy when it comes to bedtime.

"What are you eating?"

"Grapes."

"Are they good?"

"Come here and see." I pull down the covers and he crawls in. Grapes are better shared.

"What are you reading?" he asks, looking at a book I'm holding. A bestseller I don't read enough.

"It's the Bible. Do you want me to read to you?"

"Yep."

"I'm reading from a book called Matthew. Remember the song you like, 'I don't wanna be a Pharisee, 'cause they're not fair you see?' Well, one of the Pharisees asked Jesus what He wanted him to do most of all. Do you know what Jesus said?"

"What?"

"He told him to love God with everything he had, and do you know what else?"

"What?"

"He told him to love others like he loved himself. Don't you think it's more important to love others than to just tell them about Jesus? You have been telling Rachael and Jeffrey about Jesus and that makes me glad. But they need to see how kind you are to them before they'll believe what you say about Jesus. Love them, Stephen. Grown-up Christians like to talk about *contacts* and *souls*. Sometimes we sort of throw buns too, but we don't talk very often about just loving those who don't know Jesus. We need to love people until they ask us why."

My son has been silent. Undoubtedly he is impressed with my verbose rhetoric. I mean, let's face it, this has been pretty good stuff. I look over at him. His mouth is wide open, but not with awe. He is sound asleep.

Perhaps all this advice was really meant for me.

━━━━━━

Children are more likely to follow your feet than your lips.

" ─────────────────────────

Before I was married I had three theories about raising children. Now I have three children and no theories.
　　　　　　　—John Wilmot,
　　　　　　　　Earl of Rochester

Discipline... exists for the sake of what seems its very opposite—for freedom, almost for extravagance.
　　　　　　　—C.S. Lewis

You know the only people who are always sure about the proper way to raise children? Those who never had any.
　　　　　　　—Bill Cosby

Nothing is so strong as gentleness; nothing so gentle as real strength.
　　　　　　　—Ralph W. Sockman

───────────────────────── **"**

Jesus love me, dis I doe. For the Bible tell me so...." The sound filters my way from across the hall. It is six in the morning. Not just any morning: Saturday morning. Putting a pillow over my head, I manage to smile and drift off again.

"Jesus love me, dis I doe. For the Bible tell me so...." The record is stuck, and the volume is up. I put another pillow over my head.

"LITTLE ONES TO HIM BEE-ONG. THEY ARE WEAK, BUT HE IS STRONG!" I am out of pillows and patience. Sitting up, I grope for my earplugs. They are nowhere to be felt. Beside me lies my wife. Bone of my bone, flesh of my flesh. She appears to be in a deep sleep. But I'm not so sure.

The song starts again. Propping the pillows up, I lean back and listen.

It seems like only yesterday the singer was born. It was a frightening day for me. I was prepared for the process; I had been through it before. But I was unprepared for the result: the cutest little girl since, well, since my wife. Oh, I knew all about little boys. I had been one. I had had one. Boys played football. Boys spit. Boys slammed doors and made large messes in small restrooms. But little girls?

I did know one thing. Little girls were direct descendants of angels. And the last two years had confirmed my theory. Oh sure, there were times when Rachael's halo was slightly askew, like the time she hung porridge from her little brother. But a sinner she was not. Theologians may differ with me there, but I had irrefutable evidence. I had a daughter.

There, see? This girl of angelic ancestry has stopped singing and fallen asleep. I think I will, too.

———

"Rachael, we do not pour milk on the floor." It is brunch time and all is not well. My angel-daughter is staring at me, and for the first time since birth she has defiance in her eyes. She continues to drain the cup onto the floor.

"Rachael, will you obey Daddy?"

"No," she says, her halo gone.

I repeat the question. She repeats her answer: "No."

Gently removing her from the chair, I carry her down the hall to the bedroom.

Now at this point I can hear some of you just oozing advice.

> GRANDMA: "What that girl needs is a little more love."

> SOCIAL WORKER: "Whatever you do, don't spank her. Spanking is bad modeling. It teaches a child to hit others."

> GRANDPA: "Since when did a child need to be *taught* how to hit? I say you should spank the tar out of her."

> SOCIAL WORKER: "I have irrefutable evidence that spanking leads to a poor self-image. Your child may develop a negative opinion of herself—the idea that she is bad."

GRANDPA: "Well, she hasn't exactly been good."
SOCIAL WORKER: "But spanking encourages children to avoid getting caught."
GRANDPA: "Oh, come on."
GRANDMA: "I say we spank the social worker...."

"Rachael, will you obey Daddy?" I ask.

"No," she says.

An hour passes, during which I weigh much of the advice offered above. But her answer has not changed. Although her older brother is on a "just say yes" campaign outside the door, she remains defiant. I hold her, cry with her, pray for wisdom—and yes, spank her. Finally she looks at me and sniffles, "Yes, obey." In 15 minutes she is asleep in my arms.

———

It is nearing midnight now and I have just returned from playing hockey. Tiptoeing into Rachael's room, I kneel beside her bed. She is asleep. Lego blocks are scattered on the covers and in one corner Cuddle Bear rests on his head.

I stroke my daughter's blonde hair. "The Lord bless you and keep you, Rachael. The Lord make His face shine upon you and be gracious to you. The Lord turn His face toward you and give you peace. Amen."

Opening her eyes, she looks up at me. "Come," I say. She grins and reaches up.

We sit together on the couch. "I can't sleep after I play hockey, Rachael. Maybe you'll be an incurable insomniac, too." The words hold no meaning for her, but the voice does. She has followed me around the house ever since she said yes. And I have been told she "lubs" me a dozen times. Now she presses closer. As I hold her tight, I commit myself again to one of the most important of human relationships: that of a father and his daughter.

"Lord," I pray out loud, "give me wisdom and courage to bring this child up in the way she should go. Help me to be consistent in discipline and liberal in healthy affection."

I would like to say that my prayer put her to sleep. But a while after I tucked her in, she began humming. And in the morning, Daddy's little angel was singing her favorite song again. After all, it was time to get up. It was six o'clock.

Discipline is used most effectively by those who love, not those who love discipline.

4

I Can't Love Without You

"APPARENTLY I HAVE DONE SOMETHING TO UPSET YOU."

66 ——————————————————————

Basically my wife was immature. I'd be at home in the bath and she'd come in and sink my boats.
            —Woody Allen

You can give without loving but you can't love without giving.
            —Amy Carmichael

Of the seven deadly sins, anger is possibly the most fun. To lick your wounds, to smack your lips over grievances long past, to roll over your tongue the prospect of bitter confrontations still to come, to savor to the last toothsome morsel both the pain you are given and the pain you are giving back—in many ways it is a feast fit for a king. The chief drawback is that what you are wolfing down is yourself. The skeleton at the feast is you.
            —Frederick Bueckner

Write injuries in dust, benefits in marble.
            —Benjamin Franklin

——————————————————————— **99**

Hollywood Stars Falling Out of Love."
The bold headline jumps out at me from a tabloid known worldwide for its desperate pursuit of truth, accuracy, integrity, and particularly freedom of speech. Below is a celebrity couple in happier days. The photo caption reads: "We just don't love each other anymore." At the top of the page is perhaps the only truth gracing this ignominious publication—the date: August 28.

Ah, now I remember why I am standing in line surrounded by close-ups of Roseanne Barr. I am here to purchase an anniversary card. Yes, as of today Ramona and I have been married 2920 days. This afternoon we will celebrate with a round of golf and dinner alone. I can't wait!

———

"You spent *how much* on *what?*"

Two days have passed since our romantic candlelight dinner and disastrous round of golf. I am standing in the living room, hands on my hips, trying my best to look imposing.

"Forty-nine dollars on clothes."

"FORTY-NINE DOLLARS! Why didn't you tell me?" I sound angry—angrier than I am.

"I did, but you were too busy reading." She is right. I remember now.

"Uh, well..." My hands are off my hips and I am fumbling for a reply. "I just think that's a lot to spend on clothes right now."

"Pardon me?" Her voice is growing louder. Soon the neighbors will gather. "You buy things like stereos and cars and I can't even buy some clothes? WHICH WERE ON SALE?" she adds.

"I didn't say that. I just think we need to be a little more careful right now. We just had holidays, and you know we needed that car, and..."

As things heat up, I realize she is right. But there's no way I'm admitting that today.

It is time for a walk.

Down the street I smile and wave at a neighbor, but inside I am severely miffed. "Sometimes arguing with your wife is like trying to blow out a light bulb," I muse. "Especially when you're wrong."

"How are you doing, Phil?"

"Fine, thank you. Just fine." I am smiling. And lying.

What I'd really like to say is this: "Okay, so I haven't been easy to live with lately. But I'm not that bad. I don't drink away our money, or beat my wife. Maybe I feel this way because I don't love her anymore. Look, it's happening to other people. Maybe our old candle has undergone burnout too. Oh sure, I'll stay with her. But I won't speak to her for a week... maybe two. You see, I don't think I'm in love anymore."

And so that night, for the first time in over eight years of married life, I let the sun go down on our wrath.

Early the next morning she is sleeping when I leave for work.

Smooth sailing... my vow of silence is intact.

But in the office there is trouble of another kind. How does one write about family when he is so out-of-touch with his own?

Picking up my Bible, I begin reading. The book is Colossians and the text seems larger and clearer than any tabloid headline: "Clothe yourselves with compassion, kindness, humility, gentleness and patience. Bear with each other and forgive whatever grievances you may have against one another. Forgive as the Lord forgave you. And over all these virtues put on love, which binds them all together in perfect unity" (3:12-14).

Ouch!

Put on love. Not *feel* love, but choose to *do* it.

"Lord," I pray, "I'll need Your help. I'm tired of loving on my own."

Putting down my Bible I pick up the phone. "Honey? Ya, it's me. I...I'm sorry. I was wrong."

That evening things are different. We talk long into the night. We speak of love: Not an emotion. Not something we fall into. Or out of. But something we decide to do whether we feel like it or not.

The next morning I am tired, but there is a smile on my face—an honest smile. It is a good start for a husband with such a long way to go.

———

The first step to forgiveness is to admit that we don't deserve it.

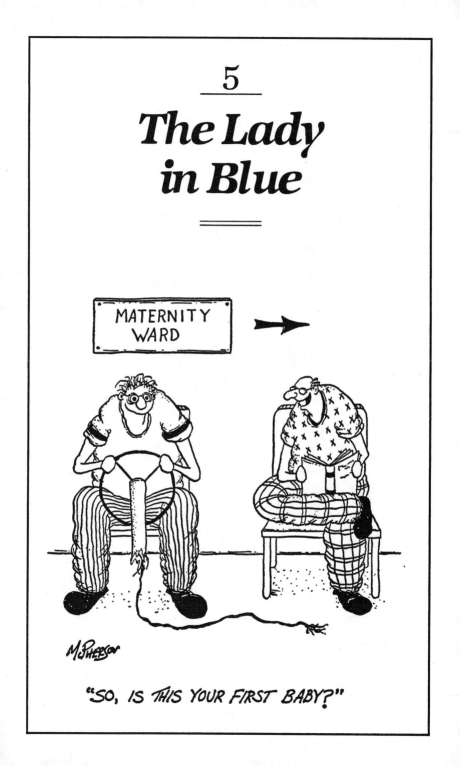

" ——————————————————————

Children are a 24-hour-a-day commitment, for a minimum of eighteen years—probably longer. With children, you can learn something very important: how to give for the sheer joy of giving. If you give to children with any hope of return you're inviting misery around.

> —John-Roger and
> Peter McWilliams

What bothers me about TV is that it tends to take our minds off our minds.

> —Robert Orben

I would never let my children even come close to this thing.

> —Vladimir Kosma Zworykin,
> Russian-born inventor of TV

I find television very educational. When it's on I go into the other room and read a book.

> —Groucho Marx

—————————————————————— **"**

I have the flu. I think doctors have dubbed it the Shanghai Swine Flu. Symptoms include everything from voice loss to a lack of enough physical stamina to hold up a paperback. These same doctors say the flu will pass, but at the moment—I wish *I* would. Painfully I muster up some energy and reach for the remote control.

Phil Donahue has just finished his opening comments, which I sadly missed, and a kind-faced lady in a blue dress turns toward the camera. Smiling she says, "The happiest day in my life will be the day my daughter leaves home. I regretted my decision to have her from day one—you know, the day she was born." Some in the audience heckle. Others applaud. Phil Donahue excitedly clutches his microphone and runs to the next aisle. His pockets jingle. The phones light up.

Ah, this is encouraging. I've finally found a few people who are even more infirmed than myself.

The director cuts back to the lady in blue. She is chewing

gum now and nervously swinging one leg. I wonder if she ever conveyed her sentiments to her daughter.

"My daughter knows how I feel. . . .We have a very open relationship." The lady continues to smile and chew gum as she says these things.

By the end of the hour, other people begin to share her sentiments. "Kids are a pain," says one person. "They're, like, so much—like—total trouble, you know?" Another woman agrees: "I'd like to get on with my life. I was a nurse two years ago; now my career's been put on hold. How can I take three steps forward with four kids holding me back?"

One newly married couple shares their incredible insight: "Parenthood is too costly; we've decided not to have kids. We'll have things like holidays instead." I wonder how these folk propose that we continue the human race.

But at the same time I begin to consider my own situation. Certainly parenting has its drawbacks. Since three kids eat up to 50 percent of any household's income, it hasn't been our best move economically. And without children I wouldn't always be stubbing my toes on toys. Or frantically searching for one shoe. And just think of the vacations we have missed. The peace and quiet. The evenings out. The weekends together—alone.

But a funny thing happened as I rested upon my self-pity: The sound of little feet came echoing down the hall. A three-year-old boy pressed through the door followed by his little sister. He was holding my dinner at an 18-degree angle. "Here's your first course, Daddy," he said. Toast and an apple had never tasted better. A few minutes later he brought my final course, sneezed on it, then took his little sister by the hand and went quietly out of the room. The whole thing was obviously choreographed by their mother.

My mind went back to the lady in blue. And although I knew I would never be able to tell about it on the Donahue show, I wondered what had been the happiest day of my life. Several memories came to mind, but none could top that of a hot May day in 1986 when I first gazed into the eyes of my son. I had seen other babies. Other babies were wrinkled and purple. But this baby was—well—wrinkled and purple, but truly beautiful. This was my son.

God had heard our prayers and given us the first of three gifts which grow more precious each day. What could be more exciting than watching him grow. Showing him how to catch a ball. Or teaching him to ice skate? And what memory could I treasure more than the first day he wrapped his arms around my neck and whispered, "Love you, Daddy"?

"Lord, thank You for the privilege of parenthood," I prayed. "For these three gifts You have entrusted us with. I give them to You again. Soon these halls will echo only with the memory of their laughter. Help us to make the most of each moment and point them to You each day."

Oh, yes. You're wondering about the Shanghai Swine Flu. Well, it's gone. It seems that I passed it on to my wife, and I just sent her dinner—in the hands of a three-year-old.

———

Great opportunities come to those who make the most of small ones.

6

Surprise, Surprise

"

God gives His gifts where He finds the vessel empty enough to receive them.

　　　　　　　　　—C.S. Lewis

Children were more to Jesus than helpless, gentle creatures to be loved and protected; they were His chief parable of the kingdom of heaven.

　　　　　　　　　—John Watson

Prayer is a cry of hope.

　　　　　　　　　—French Proverb

The quickest way to get back on your feet is to get down on your knees.

　　　　　　　　　—Vern McLellan

"

It is midnight. In the Western Hemisphere children are sleeping. Lullabies have been sung. Prayers said. I am just settling down for a short winter's nap when down the hall comes the sound of muffled footsteps. Slowly they draw near.

Burglars?

In that no-man's-land between consciousness and sleep, the worst becomes the possible. My heart skips a beat and I am wide awake.

Silently our door swings open.

In the soft glow of a night-light stands a lone figure. He is approximately three feet tall and is smiling around his soother. His name is Jeffrey Paul. A pillow hangs like his sister's doll from his left hand, and from his right, a pail of Lego blocks. For a two-year-old who can't spell *schedule*, it is time to play.

"Come," I whisper.

Setting down the pail, he clutches the pillow and climbs

in. Putting one arm across my chest, he lets out an excited squeak.

"Daddy, I afwaid," he says. *Ah, Jeff, I wouldn't trade you for all the beans in Boston. But, I'm ashamed to say, it wasn't always that way....*

Date: September 30, 1988.
Location: The dinner table.

"Honey, I think...um...well, I think I just might be... uh, *pregnant*." My wife was talking with my mouth full. Resisting a choking reflex, I took a quick drink, swallowed the potatoes, and calmly responded, "WHAT? THAT'S IMPOSSIBLE! RACHAEL IS THREE DAYS OLD!"

"Three *months* old," she corrected me.

"But it can't be. You're joking, aren't you? Ha, you're joking." I looked at her closely. She wasn't joking. Husbands know these things.

"I was just starting to feel like I could get up in the morning...." Her words were distant.

I stabbed another potato...hard.

"Three kids in three years!" Her words were getting closer: "And I was looking forward to some things: sleep, peace—even the holidays."

Date: June 29, 1989.
Location: Maternity ward, local hospital.

Thirty-three weeks had passed since our dinner-table conversation. Gathered with us to witness this most private of events was the obstetrician, the pediatrician, the anesthesiologist, the janitor, the janitor's understudy, the taxi driver, and three premed students. But we really didn't notice. You see, Jeffrey Paul had just been born. He came into the world much like our other two, but you didn't need a grade-eight education to determine he would be very different. From week one Jeffrey let us know, long into the night, that he was not pleased to be here. No, this was not his decision, and someone else should pay.

His whimper could melt your heart, but his piercing howl could peel wallpaper. "He's colicky," explained my wife. "I was when I was his age, and your mother says you were, too." Having access to this information did not help.

By the time he learned to use a soother, another problem had arisen: Jeffrey was—well—aggressive. Some people would call him strong-willed, impossible even. If he wanted something, he would flag down a freight train to get it. This became frighteningly evident long before the day we stood in a cafeteria line and watched him reach out and hit a total stranger, perhaps for the sheer joy of watching her bend over to rub her knee.

"Do you suppose we got the wrong one?" I ventured that night. "You know, sometimes the baskets get swapped."

"Naw," my wife responded. "He's too much like you."

She was right.

Born of parents who were beginning to resemble Abraham and Sarah (not just in faith), I was politely referred to as the caboose. An afterthought. A mistake. But I never heard those words from them. Instead, I heard words like, "I love you" and, "I don't know what I would do without you." And, just as importantly, I was shown that love. I was loved, just like the rest.

And so, my son, it will be with you. Not because it's all I know or because it's the noble thing, but because God's grace always accompanies His surprises. And because it's true: I can't imagine life without you. Life without your "Wock me, Dad." Life without your smile.

But now it's time for bed. Jeffrey picks up his Lego pail. I gather his pillow and we head for the crib. "Goodnight, Jeff; I love you."

"Lub you, too," he says. *Ah, these are great days.*

Back in bed I drift off, when again down the hall comes the sound of muffled footsteps. Slowly they draw near. Burglars? I don't think so.

———

When opportunity knocks, the pessimist usually complains about the noise.

7

Three Men and a Lawnmower

"LOOKS LIKE THAT MOWER OF YOURS STARTS A LITTLE HARD."

" ————————————————————

Keep your friendships in repair.
                    —Ralph Waldo Emerson

*The holy passion of Friendship is of so sweet
and steady and loyal and enduring a nature
that it will last through a whole life-time, if not
asked to lend money.*
                    —Mark Twain

*I like long walks, especially when they are
taken by people who annoy me.*
                    —Fred Allen

A friend loves at all times.
                    —Solomon

———————————————————— **"**

I would like to think I'm a nineties kind of guy: Sensitive. Caring. Able to help out in the kitchen. Able to change diapers which are beyond the point of being recycled. Able to laugh at my past mistakes—and scalp those who join me.

But I must tell you, I'm not a fan of these back-to-nature weekend groups where men pay hard-earned cash to sit around a fire, thump their chests, and chant catchy slogans—all in the hope that they will bond before they are attacked by rabid grizzly bears. Instead, I have found Christian friendships celebrated around backyard barbecues, long walks, and late-night discussions to be the stuff real men are made of.

I sincerely hope these celebrations continue. For, you see, after what happened a few months ago, I have cause for concern.

It all started the day my new neighbor introduced himself. "Hi," he said, smiling winsomely, "I'm Vance. May I borrow your toolbox?" So began a meaningful relationship which has grown with the passing of time—and food, tapes, catalogs, books, even articles of clothing. Yes, within one month of moving in, Vance had, at least once, borrowed almost every item in my house including my new Reeboks, which don't come close to fitting him.

Yet if I sound bitter, it is not the case. No, you see, Vance is the kind of neighbor everyone dreams about having. For Vance owns a lawnmower that works.

I have owned an electric one myself for some time now, but it was never, even in its prime, very healthy. In fact, each time I plugged it in I was guaranteed higher ratings than Monday Night Football. People would come from other time zones to see what the noise was.

> RUSSIAN HUSBAND: "Wow, honey. Did you hear that? I'll bet it's that Callaway guy's lawn-mower again."
> RUSSIAN WIFE: "Really? I thought it was coming from Chernobyl."

Yes, with the flip of one switch I could cause a power surge that would turn lights off all over town. So, in the interest of things like world peace, I relegated it to a garage sale where I attached a sign: "Used Lawnmower. Needs Some Work."

Then I borrowed Vance's.

This, I knew, would not be a problem because if one calculated the total net worth of the products being exchanged (and far be it from me to ever, ever do this), one would discover that I had every right to borrow expensive farm implements.

After clearing my yard of enough trucks, dolls, wagons, and balls to open a competitive toy-store chain and firmly inserting my fluorescent-orange earplugs, I gave the lawnmower two swift pulls.

It started.

Looking back now, I realize I should have shut it off right then. I should have removed the earplugs. I should have pushed the mower back to Vance's shed. Instead, I proceeded to trim our backyard.

Everything was moving along quite well—until I reached The Stump. A lawnmower this powerful should clear The Stump with no problem, I reasoned, the earplugs clearly blocking the flow of anything at all to my brain area. Besides, anything sticking an inch-and-a-half out of the ground could be hazardous to your children and should be trimmed.

Baaaang! Then nothing.

I tried the pull-start mechanism. It wouldn't pull. So, I followed the advice my parents had faithfully drummed into me so many years ago. "Philip," they had said, "when you borrow something, always return it."

I returned it. Vance was gone at the time but, I reasoned, it would start when he tried it. Besides, Vance has mechanical abilities. He would be able to borrow some tools and fix it.

Then I went across the street to my new neighbor Jim's house.

Now Jim is known on our block for his pretty fair lawnmower but, more than that, his ability to keep a good secret.

"You won't believe this," I told him. "I hit a stump."

"You're telling me?" he replied, rolling his eyes. "They heard it in Cairo."

"Uh, do you mind if I borrow *your* lawnmower?"

"Sure," he replied, "Or shall we just destroy it together right here in *my* yard?"

A week later, upon returning from a business trip, I found Vance waiting.

"Hi," I said, trying not to show my nervousness.

"Howdy," he replied, grinning one of those I-know-something-you-hope-I-don't grins. "Do you mind if I borrow your flashlight?"

Whew, I thought. *All is well. All is normal.* "Sure thing. I'll get it."

And I did. But when I handed him the flashlight, Vance motioned with his hand and said, "Come with me."

Now you must understand that Vance is bigger than I. In fact, comparatively speaking, one of us plays rugby, the other rides race horses. We had just begun the slow walk out to my backyard when Vance turned and began to club me on the head with the flashlight. Slowly I sank to my knees in the darkness. No, not really. But I sincerely wondered if he would pummel me. Instead, Vance led me to The Stump. And this is the truth: Surrounding The Stump was a "Police Line Do Not Cross" yellow ribbon. And on the ground below was a white-painted outline of a lawnmower.

"We have a suspect," smiled Vance.

"What do you mean *we?*"

"Jim and me."

Then he took me to the garden, where all that protruded from a small mound of earth was a stainless-steel lawnmower handlebar. A large gray brick marked the spot. Etched upon the brick was this eulogy:

Here lies Mr. Mower
1982-1992
A hand so quickly taken
by a hand so quick to take.
He will never mow
what life had
in the grass ahead of him.

I don't know what your friends are like but, believe it or not, I sincerely wish for you friends like mine. Friends like Paul, Kevin, Gord, Conrad—even Jim and Vance. Friends I can pray with. Friends I can laugh with. Friends who walk in when others walk out. Friends who care enough to face me with the truth about myself. And yes, friends who are able to forgive.

Well, it's time to close this chapter. Besides, I really better go. Someone's at the door. It's probably Vance. Perhaps he wants to borrow something. Or, he's here for the next payment on that new lawnmower.

———

A man is known by the enemies he makes.

" ———————————————————————————————

Marriages are made in heaven, but they are lived on earth.
—George P. Weiss

God help the man who won't marry until he finds the perfect woman, and God help him still more if he finds her.
—Benjamin Tillett

The Christian religion, by confining marriage to pairs, and rendering the relation indissoluble, has by these two things done more toward the peace, happiness, settlement, and civilization of the world, than by any other part in this whole scheme of divine wisdom.
—Edmund Burke

——————————————————————————————— **"**

I think I'm going crazy," says Ramona. From my spot in the kitchen, her voice seems to emanate from a pile of laundry that consists largely of recyclable diapers.

"Why would you want to do that?" I ask. "I know some mothers with *seven* kids who would trade you jobs any day." It is not a good joke. My timing is bad and the laundry pile does not respond.

Four years ago we had enjoyed our last vacation alone. We laughed, talked, slept, and golfed together. But standing in the kitchen today I feel like we haven't seen each other since.

"Shall we go to the Bahamas?" I say half-jokingly. "We could borrow the money from your parents." I am no longer joking.

"Well, we need to do something," says the laundry.

Twenty-four hours later we are driving toward the nearest city—not to the airport, but to a hotel with a Great-Escape Weekend rate.

"Will that be a table for two, sir?"

"Yes. Just two." It is hard to believe.

"Smoking or nonsmoking?"

"The breathing section, please," I say. Our host is not amused. I should have noticed the blue-and-white box in his shirt pocket.

Once we are seated, we look around. "This is nice," says Ramona. What she really means is, "I don't see any high chairs or bibs. Just a bunch of adults and a table for two." She is right.

We sit in silence, looking at each other over two yellow roses. I like the way her eyes reflect the candlelight.

"I still can't believe you fell for me," I whisper with a grin.

She smiles.

If the truth were told, it was I who did the falling. We laugh as I begin to recall a very special ski trip seven years earlier. The day I first fell in love...literally.

––––––––––

If you've ever been foolish enough to try out a big ski hill in Canada's Rocky Mountains, you know that, in addition to coaxing your skis to cooperate, you must face several other obstacles, not the least of which is The Chair Lift.

The Chair Lift at Lake Louise looks perfectly harmless at the bottom of the mountain, but what bothers people like myself (who have fairly good eyesight) is that you can't see where the chair lift ends. For all you know, people who climb aboard are never heard from again.

Headline: "Chair Lift Claims Record Number of Eager Skiers."

But believing that this many tourists could not be wrong, I followed my potential relatives-in-law and joined the long line of eager skiers awaiting The Chair Lift. Or, let's be accurate here, I came close to activating the insurance policies of about a dozen of them.

After brushing myself off and offering my condolences, I awkwardly climbed aboard The Chair Lift. While ascending the mountain, it never occurred to me that, should we ever reach our destination, I had no idea how to disembark. My potential relatives-in-law, and the one I was hoping to impress, had gone on ahead, leaving me to learn by experiment.

"He ice-skates pretty good," I heard one of them say. "He shouldn't have much trouble with this."

"Ski Tips Up," shouted the sign. I put my ski tips up. Then I watched the strangers disembark. It looked easy enough. But by the time I had finished admiring their style, the distance to the ground required a bungee cord, and to top it off, the chair was still moving. So I took the next logical step. Turning around, I let myself slowly slide off and grabbed onto the front of the chair. From this unique vantage point, I watched the ground move further and further from my skis.

I wonder if they can shut this thing off, I thought. *If not, this will be a mighty uncomfortable way to ride down the mountain.* As the lift controller began to shout at high decibels words which it would be unwise for me to reprint here, I did the thing that people with cords hooked to their legs pay $59.95 to do: I jumped.

It is difficult to say how much time passed before I hit the ground, surrounded by skiers with open mouths.

Then I heard her laugh. How I loved her laugh!

Was it that funny, or was she just glad I was alive? I wasn't sure. In fact, I wasn't quite sure if I *was* alive. But clearly I had left some sort of impression, and as she came over to help me up, I realized I was falling head over heels in love.

Had I known that I stood a much better chance of getting to the bottom of the hill alive than I did of marrying this girl, I might have asked to be put back on The Chair. But 11 years later, as I reach across the table and take her hand, I am so glad I hadn't done that.

Ramona takes a flower from the vase and holds it to my nose. Across the room another couple watches us suspiciously, perhaps wondering if we are in the midst of some illicit affair. After all, married people don't act like that, do they?

"It's great to be in love with your wife," I tell her. "And it keeps getting better."

She smiles. "For me, too."

In the early days of our marriage I often wondered how we would make it: endless arguments... angry nights when there seemed to be no solution... a clash of wills... two selfish kids trying to make sense of a lifetime commitment. But the thing that neither of us would contemplate was divorce. The word did not enter our vocabulary. Some would say we were stuck with each other. Imprisoned. But I believe it provided us the time, and God the opportunity, to create a better thing between us.

Later that night in the darkness of a strange hotel we thank God for His mercy, and I go to sleep with a smile on my face. After all, it's great being married to your best friend—especially when you started out going downhill.

———

In tennis love is nothing;
in marriage love is everything.

9

Of Bedtime and Three-Year-Olds

"I'LL BE THERE IN A SECOND DEAR. I'M TUCKING THE KIDS IN."

" ———————————————————————

When I approach a child, he inspires in me two sentiments: tenderness for what he is, and respect for what he may become.

        —Louis Pasteur

Borrowed beliefs have no power.

        —James Black

——————————————————————— **"**

Bedtime is story time at our house. On most nights you will find three children and their father on the couch, sometimes sharing a blanket, but always sharing a book. Tonight I have just finished a story in Numbers 16 wherein the ground opens up and the families of Korah, Dathan, and Abiram are—well, let's be honest here—emphatically squashed.

According to several behavioral scientists, this is extremely harmful stuff. Imagine the lasting damage that will be done to the psyches of young, impressionable children. The Bible is violent. It should be banned, they say, in their expensive reports. Then they go home and watch Stephen King reruns.

On this night the behavioral scientists seem to be wrong. Within minutes of reading the story, and partly due to the serenading of Michael Card's "Sleep Sound in Jesus," Rachael and Jeffrey have fallen asleep.

But perhaps the scientists would prefer to study Stephen. He is still wide awake and can't seem to get enough of Korah, Dathan, and Abiram.

"Daddy, tell me the story about the Israel guys again. Could ya? Tell me, 'kay?" Stephen's eyes have every reason to be shut. His light is out. His cassette is on. His head rests gently against a stuffed raccoon. But his father is beside him on his favorite chair. "Daddy, tell me about those Israel guys who got swallowed by the dirt."

"Okay. Let's see..."

"And tell me about when I was in Mommy's tummy."

"Alright. It was about four years ago now. Mommy and I were in bed one night. I was almost asleep when all of a sudden you kicked me in the back."

"What?" His eyes widen. He lets out a squeak and laughs. It is a story he never tires of. "I kicked you in the back?"

"Yes, and I jumped almost clear to the ceiling. Then Mommy and I felt her tummy. You kicked some more and we prayed for you just like we had done lots of other nights. We thanked God for you and we asked Him for a healthy baby. And most of all we prayed that you would grow up to love Jesus."

"Then was I borned?" He is squeezing Mr. 'Coon.

"Not yet. The next thing you did was go to sleep. But Mommy didn't. In fact she didn't sleep at all that night. I made up for it, though. I slept while she paced the floor.

"When she woke me the next morning, I knew it was time to go to the hospital. You had decided that you'd like to see what was going on in the big old world."

"What about the baseball guys?"

"Well, when we arrived, I couldn't believe it. There was a baseball tournament going on right across from the hospital. Had these guys no respect at all? I mean, a baby was about to be born.

"But that night at 6:04 I put a perfectly formed little baby into Mommy's arms. I'll never understand how she was able to smile after all that, but I've never seen her happier. God had given us a baby boy."

"That was me."

"Yes, that was you. As I stood there, I thought of the many parents who didn't want their babies. And I remembered the verses in the Bible that say, 'You formed me in my mother's body. I praise You because You made me in an amazing and wonderful way....You saw my bones being formed as I took shape....All the days planned for me were written in Your book before I was one day old.'"

"We wanted you, Stephen, and we still thank God for you every day."

He is smiling again. Both arms surround Mr. 'Coon. "Are you going to work tomorrow?" he asks.

"Yes."

"Then I shall be sad."

"Don't be sad; I'll be back for dinner."

"Will you run away?"

"No, Stephen."

"Some daddies run away."

"Who told you that?"

"I don't know. Somebody said that their daddy ran away and stayed gone."

"No, I won't ever run away. I love Mommy and I love you kids too much to run away. Goodnight, Stephen. I love you." I kiss his forehead and stand to leave.

He closes his eyes. "'Night," he says.

I move down the hall to check on his sister.

"Daddy?" Stephen is calling again.

"Yes?"

"Is Jesus under my bed?"

"Jesus is with you always, Stephen."

"If Jesus is under my bed then the woozul can't get me."

"The woozul can't get you. Goodnight now. It's time to sleep."

"Daddy?"

"Yes, Stephen?"

"You forgot to tell me about the Israel guys."

═══════

It is easier to build a boy than to repair a man.

10

False Teeth and Funny Bones

"ARE YOU TRYING TO DESTROY MY SOCIAL LIFE?! I KNOW PEOPLE AROUND HERE, DAD! PLEASE TAKE OFF THAT STUPID HAT!"

"

When I became a man I put away childish things, including the fear of childishness and the desire to be grown up.

—C.S. Lewis

Why can't we buy just one airplane and have all the pilots take turns?

—Calvin Coolidge,
Thirtieth President of
the United States

Oh God, may I live to have one day of unsullied joy!

—Ludwig van Beethoven

If you have no joy...there's a leak in your Christianity somewhere.

—Billy Sunday

My grandmother started walking five miles a day when she was sixty. She's ninety-five now, and we don't know where...she is.

—Ellen Degeneria

"

You should have seen the look on my friend's face. Moments before we had been playing quietly on the floor. Now he was standing in the middle of our living room, his mouth wide open, his eyes wide, his lower lip resting on his new white tennis shoes. The object of his horror: my father.

Dad, in an effort to imitate someone who could make a serious bid for the Frankenstein role in an upcoming film, had just come into the room, crossed his eyes, and lowered his false teeth.

Oh no! I thought. *How embarrassing! Now everyone will know! Dad, how could you?*

I knew what my friend was thinking. He was asking himself the same questions a few other startled friends of mine had asked a zillion times before: Did this man really start his sojourn under our ozone layer? Does his steering wheel turn the tires? And his hotel, does it have a thirteenth floor?

These questions were not surprising when one considered the questionee. Raised in a home where laughter was located under "L" in the dictionary but rarely displayed elsewhere, he was shocked to finally meet an adult whose funny bone was not in a cast.

Standing beside my open-mouthed friend who looked to be preparing passage for an antiaircraft carrier, I vowed then and there to provide a *normal* home for my offspring. My children would feel safe at our house. Yesiree. Their friends could come and play freely—without embarrassment. My home would be a haven *from* mirth and merriment.

But I was only eight. What does an eight-year-old know about the meaning of the word *hereditary*?

By the time my wife and I had 3 little blessings from above (in as many short years), it became apparent that a sense of humor was more to be desired than baldness on the list of things I had inherited. If you disagree, I invite you to take triplets down a waterslide.

TRIPLETS: "Boy, this is fun."
YOU: "Aaaahhhh!"

Just last Saturday, my son's friend Joel came to visit and, like all small, sensitive boys who intuitively know when tired adults are resting, he attacked the door with both fists.

ME (after opening the door): "Hi, Joel."
JOEL (holding a sharp stick): "Mr. Callaway, can I play with Stephen?"
ME (looking at the stick): "Sure."
JOEL (poking an ant with the stick): "Where is he?"
ME (trying to gently confiscate the stick): "He's up on the roof eating a banana."
JOEL (after backing up far enough to see that Stephen isn't on the roof): "I don't see him."
ME: "Well, he'll probably be down in a minute. I think he'll slide down on the peel."
JOEL (dropping the stick and moving further back, yelling from the street): "I still don't see him."

STEPHEN (standing behind me now): "Hi, Joel."
JOEL (picking up the stick, shouting loudly): "Mr. Callaway, you were just joking me!"

Of course, this sense-of-humor thing can be carried too far. My wife gets the biggest enjoyment out of things that aren't funny at all. Take, for instance, the day she almost cashed in on my insurance policy.

After a rather tough day at the office, I was looking forward to a peaceful evening at home—changing diapers and playing with three tornadoes. All I had to do was navigate the last turn into our yard while carrying a large, black briefcase full of hardback books. I suppose it did not help that I was on a bicycle. Of course you know what happened: My front tire got caught between the lawn and the sidewalk and I was catapulted unceremoniously into the bushes.

It must have looked quite hilarious from the house, because moments later the one who loves me more than life itself stood over me laughing quite uproariously.

"Are you okay?" she asked as she breathed deeply and tried not to hyperventilate.

"Oh, I'm fine. It's just my right leg," I replied. "It's nothing a good surgeon can't set. And the teeth ... hey, I'll get a plate made."

From inside the house three children were watching our quality time together, their runny little noses pressed up closer to the windowpane than to their own faces. "Ha, Daddy funny."

I'm not sure how much of this particular brand of humor I want our kids to inherit. But I do know this: I will be forever grateful for parents who passed on the gift of laughter. For a family who taught me to view the funny in the ordinary.

And somehow, strange though it may seem, I have always found it easier to accept the serious from the lips of the lighthearted. Perhaps that had something to do with the reason I knelt by my bed when I was five years old to do something millions of other people had done before. I had heard the message of a Savior who loved me enough to die for me from someone I had no reason not to believe absolutely. From a mother who felt that the best thing she could do in British Columbia, after discovering she had left her false teeth beneath a picnic table in Washington, was to laugh.

—————

Laugh lots, and when you grow old all your
wrinkles will be in the right places.

"

My ancestors told me to have many children.
> —Thuma Nzumakase,
> Father of 139

The best opportunities belong to those parents who will confess their faults to their children; there is no way so straight and sure to their hearts.
> —Jeremy Taylor

There is no more influential or powerful role on earth than a mother's.
> —Charles Stanley

The private work is the great one and the public work the small.
> —G.K. Chesterton

"

Leaning back in the chair, I put my hands behind my head and closed my eyes. One more hour and the holidays would be here. I tried to envision the three weeks ahead.

Ah, it would be wonderful!

Although we wouldn't be going far (my wife was in the final stages of pregnancy and in a sour mood whenever I mentioned the drive to Alaska), I would finally be able to spend some quantity time with my preschoolers. I would take them swimming, shopping, to the zoo, to the lake. They would sit and watch me as I worked on the car and cut the grass. They would help me weed the garden. Aaah, vacation! There was nothing quite like it. My lucky wife spent seven days a week at home with these little darlings.

Finally, it was my turn.

Things started out pretty well. On our first evening together, I took the kids out for ice cream and they got some in their mouths. But when we arrived home, Ramona informed me that it might be a good idea for us to go to the hospital—right this very minute! I remained perfectly calm.

After all, this was not the first time we had gone through this ordeal.

"It's okay, it's okay," I assured her. "I will be fine."

After seven hours—which rate right up there with barefoot ice-fishing—our third child was born. Although I applauded my wife and the miracle of birth, as I drove to pick up our other two angels from their grandparents' house, I wondered again if there wasn't a better way of reproducing. "Certain types of worms merely separate," I said out loud.

That night there was cause for celebration. After the angels were in bed, a friend dropped by to commemorate with me the birth of our third-born. 7-Up, peanuts, and a good movie were the order of the evening, but by the time I went to bed I was thinking, "It's a good thing I'm on holidays. I shall need a little rest."

As I dozed off, visions of summer sun danced through my head. Visions of that special trip to the zoo. That boat ride on the lake. Visions of . . . suddenly, there he was.

"Time to get up, Dad."

"Whaaat? Where are we? Who are we? Who are *you?* What time is it?"

I groped for the clock. It was 7 A.M. I had slept four hours.

Breakfast: a meal with my kids . . . time to get to know each other . . . quantity time. Rachael, our one-year-old, smiled at me past three teeth. She was so sweet. Her pink bib was so clean. *Boys are messy,* I thought. *Imagine, a clean bib.* Rachael continued to smile at me as she deposited her bowl of soggy Cheerios on the floor. I smiled back. Three-year-old Stephen promptly dropped his piece of bread on the floor, jam-side down. "But . . . Daddy," was all he said.

"That's okay."

Then he spilled his milk.

"But . . . Daddy."

By this time I thought we could all use a little fresh air, so off we went—shopping. Now, I will confess that in years past I have been highly critical of supermarket mothers. Especially those with more than one child in their shopping cart.

Especially those who have had enough of the screaming and "accidentally" swapped carts with other unsuspecting shoppers. By the time we reached the checkout counter, I was looking (and feeling) just like one of these moms.

"What's that hanging from your cart, Mr. Callaway?"

"Oh, that's my oldest child."

"No, no. The red sticky stuff."

On the way home, Rachael remembered that she didn't appreciate being strapped into a car seat. Without a good set of earplugs, a trip to the zoo would be impossible. By nightfall I was exhausted, and I hadn't even done the dishes. Or swept the floor. Or cleaned the house.

The next day dawned early. Again. I wondered why kids didn't just sleep half the morning. I used to. When I was in high school.

Following another adventuresome breakfast, I put on a children's video and instructed the kids to watch quietly while Daddy rested on the living room floor. It was not a good idea. Fathers in that position should keep their *eyes* open. Mine were closed. Just as I began to doze off, Rachael brought her soggy diaper to rest on Daddy's head.

Nightfall brought with it the promise of much-needed sleep. But it was not to be. Rachael wouldn't go to sleep. Daddy couldn't find her soother, and he was being punished.

I looked everywhere—twice. Finally I found it in the heat vent. When I brought it to her, she was fast asleep.

"What does Jesus look like?" asked Stephen. *This is not the time,* I thought. *Can't he see Daddy is tired? Questions like this are to be asked after church. Or after a good dinner.* I lay down beside him. This was the time for questions at our house.

"When will Mommy come home?"

"Soon," I answered. "Just two more sleeps." Then I began to confess my sins to a three-year-old: "Before I came home for holidays, I thought Mommy's work was easy. But then I saw the mess you two make, and how many diapers need changing. Would you like to make the beds, wash the clothes, make meals, clean the house, and change diapers?"

He screwed up his little nose.

"I'm thankful for Mommy," I continued. "I had no idea how hard she works."

He nodded. "She loves Jesus."

"Let's thank Him for her." I prayed out loud asking God's forgiveness for taking my wife for granted, and thanking Him for her hard work, her unselfish love.

When I looked over at Stephen, he was sound asleep.

And now it was my turn. On my way to the bedroom I took one last look into Rachael's room. She was standing up in her crib smiling at me. And looking for her soother.

———

If evolution was true, mothers would have more than two hands.

12

The In-laws Are Coming! The In-laws Are Coming!

" ————————————————————————

*My idea of an agreeable person is a person
who agrees with me.*
                    —Benjamin Disraeli

*When all men think alike, they are not thinking
at all.*
                    —A. Clutton Brock

*Five great enemies of peace inhabit with us—
avarice, ambition, envy, anger, and pride; if
these were to be banished, we should infallibly
enjoy perpetual peace.*
                    —Petrarch

*Mother-in-law: A woman who is never
outspoken.*
                    —Bob Phillips

———————————————————————— **"**

I recall well the day we first discussed the in-law problem. As a 19-year-old to whom much wisdom had been entrusted, I made it unmistakably clear to my potential wife that we would be marrying *each other*, not any of each other's immediate relatives.

"We will live in different towns, cities, or countries from them," I tactfully told her. "And should one of them choose to move into a town, city, or country which is in or near one in which we are inhabitants, we will distance ourselves with a U-Haul or," and this I voiced most emphatically, "I will eat my shirt or an entire wardrobe, for that matter."

She only smiled at my words.

Then the most surprising thing happened: She agreed to marry me. And following a blissful honeymoon, we found ourselves living in a small town which was quite peaceful and also largely in-law-free.

But as is often the case with those who vow to refrain from eating things disdained, they inevitably end up chewing upon those things, and sometimes even savoring them. In my case, it happened something like this...

We had friends who had them. We had seen them in photo albums, at stoplights, in strollers. And besides, it seemed like a good idea at the time. So we decided to have children.

Four years later we became the proud parents of a little boy. We were told we could name him, and so we did. People brought gifts and generally drooled when they saw him. "He's so cute," they would say sweetly. Then they would look at me, comparing. "Wow, this child is REALLY cute. How did this child get to be so cute?" Other than that, it was all quite fun. Not so much fun at the outset for Ramona, I'll admit, but nevertheless fun for me.

Then several complications set in. For one thing, it soon became apparent that my wife would not be playing beach volleyball for a few weeks, nor would she be cooking or cleaning the house, which until now had been her custom.

"So what's for supper?" she would ask from our water-bed where she was feeding the youngest member of the household, and of course wishing to be fed herself.

"I'll boil some water and we can have some . . . uh, what goes good with water?" I would say.

"Soup," came the answer.

"I think I'll order pizza."

Laughter came from the waterbed. "Don't worry," said she, "someone is coming tomorrow to help you out."

"And who," I questioned, "might that someone be?"

"My mother," said she.

I had heard and exchanged a zillion mother-in-law jokes, and I knew there was a plant with sharp leaves known as Mother-in-law's Tongue. But I was altogether unprepared for what would happen to my preconceived notions during the following week.

In the space of a few short days, I gained a new appreciation for one who had raised seven children alone after her husband had drowned trying to save one of them. Someone whose faith in God had grown through trials I could know little of. Besides, it's hard not to appreciate one who could take a squealing newborn from a rookie father and moments later bring him face-to-face with some of the best ham and roast beef in the world.

Ah, there's no one in the world quite like Grandma.

Six years have come and gone since my change of heart. And during that time "Mom" has moved to where she can now reach us toll-free. In fact, about once a month she cuts my hair. Yes, I know it sounds like the makings for a good episode of "Alfred Hitchcock Presents," but it is the truth. It is a strange sensation, the sharp scissors cutting so close to my ears. But for me it is a monthly lesson in trust—and perhaps from her the ultimate display of self-control.

During these six years I have listened to others who decided to get along without certain members of their families. But I think that's a little like deciding you don't like your left leg and can get along without it. Oh sure, you may learn to walk again, but I believe you will always be missing out on something.

In my case, I wouldn't be the only one missing out. When the grandparents arrive at our house, the children can hardly contain their excitement. They descend from the rafters with squeals of delight to be hugged, baby-sat, read to, and spoiled.

It might have cost me my shirt, but I wouldn't want it any other way.

———

Should your ship come in, it will undoubtedly be laden with relatives.

13

Honey, I Dunked the Kids

"————————————————

Joy in living comes from immersion in something one recognizes to be bigger, better, worthier, more enduring than he himself is. True happiness and true freedom come from squandering one's self for a purpose.
>   —Carl W. McGeehon

Every man brings an egg and every one wants an omelette—but without breaking his own egg. That poses a most difficult situation.
>   —Frank Mar

He who falls in love with himself will have no rivals.
>   —Benjamin Franklin

————————————————— **"**

For most of us, the mailbox provides a welcome reprieve from normalcy. It is the one moment in the day that promises the unexpected. That moment when friends long-forgotten may write, when bills come, when creditors threaten, and when *Reader's Digest* informs us that, boy oh boy, we've just won *another* $11 million.

Upon opening my mailbox on this May day, the first item to fall out was a flyer proclaiming, "Horizon Bed and Breakfast. Come and join us." Nestled deep in the heart of the Canadian Rockies, the flyer boasted, was a little cabin. This little cabin was near a lake, near a beach, near a waterslide, and near lots of food. All of these things tantalized me.

"What do you think?" I asked my wife upon arriving home.

"I think it's a great idea," she said. "And after last year, you sure could use a rest."

So I dialed the number.

"Yes, we have a vacancy in July," said the voice in my earpiece. "What's that? Oh sure. Bring the kids. They'll love

87

it here. We're on a small farm. There are some cows, some swings.... What's that? No, no bears. At least I haven't seen any bears. HAVE YOU SEEN ANY BEARS, HONEY? No, no bears. Cows, though.... What's that? Oh, I think so. IS THE HOUSE CHILDPROOF, HONEY? Yes, it's childproof. We've had kids stay here before. Besides, we have grand-children, you know."

"We'll take it."

Hanging the phone up, I turned to my wife. "It's child-proof. You know, like Fort Knox. Or Alcatraz."

Upon July's arrival, our family of five could be found heading toward our cozy, childproof cabin in the mountains, the parents conversing in typical parents-who-are-heading-off-on-holidays fashion:

HIM: "Uh, honey, did we forget anything?"
HER: "Like what?"
HIM: "Like diapers?"
HER: "No. We brought diapers."
HIM: "What about extra diapers?"
HER: "Yep. We brought extra diapers."
HIM: "What about extra thick diapers?"
HER: "Yep. Extra thick diapers."
HIM: "Uh, games? Cassettes? Books? Lego
        blocks? Stuffed animals? Sliced apples?"
HER: "Yep."
HIM: "What about the kids? Did we bring the
        kids?"

As night fell we arrived in what is truly one of the most beautiful places on earth. "Horizon Bed and Breakfast," said the sign, "For the Rest of Your Life." It was too dark to read the fine print, so we made up our own: "A place where mothers can leave all the fuss behind. A place where fathers can come to—well, for one thing—sleep in." But the morn-ing after our arrival we found this to be untrue.

Crash! The sound awakens me and I run downstairs. Rachael, our two-year-old, is okay, but she is looking up at me with one of those smiles which children, from the dawn of time, have been manufacturing for the moment. (A recent study has conclusively proven that no parent has ever been fooled by The Guilty Grin. It has also been conclusively proven that each child believes he will change the results of this survey.)

"What happened, Rachael?"

"Nuffin."

But behind her is evidence that something *did* happen. Behind her are the shattered pieces of a priceless cowboy statue. A priceless statue which can now be purchased quite reasonably. This is one of those moments when parents ask clever questions like, "What were you doing?"

"Bang!" She uses her hands to tell me.

Now it is one thing to smash priceless things at home, but when you are a guest...

"It looks like we just bought a statue," I say out loud.

Back in our room I am angry. Very angry. Eight hours on the road and a short night have left us all a little run-down. Now this. Somehow it must be my wife's fault, and I let her know.

"I've looked forward to this holiday for weeks, and now look what happens! Those things are worth hundreds of dollars!"

"Why are you blaming me?"

"I thought you were watching her."

"I was," she explains. "But I didn't see her reach for it."

"Okay, okay. I just thought this place was childproof."

"Phil, you're always like this on holidays. Why don't you relax? Lighten up a little. We're going to have breakfast, then go to the waterslide."

Ah, yes, the waterslide. What can go wrong at a waterslide?

―――――――

"Ramona, why don't you get us some ice cream? I'll take care of the kids." We have spent an hour in the sun, but my words are still ice-cold.

At this particular waterslide, there are three shallow pools for kids: one at the top, one at the bottom, and one in between. Each is surrounded by white rocks and all are connected by short slides. "Stephen," I say to my eldest, "you take Rachael and Jeffrey to the top pool and send them down the slide. I'll catch them." General Phil is barking orders.

"Okay," my son says. It sounds simple enough.

Standing in the bottom pool, water up to my knees, I almost enjoy the sight of the three of them going hand-in-hand up the sidewalk. When they arrive at the top pool I yell, "Alright, let her go!"

Stephen picks Rachael up and lets her go—down the wrong slide! I lunge from the pool, run over the rocks, and jump to catch her—just in time. She is grinning from ear to ear. The lifeguard is shouting, "Hey, you there. Stay off the rocks."

"Daddy, funny," Rachael says. I see nothing humorous whatsoever.

Looking up I notice that Stephen is now placing his little brother in the *other* slide. "No, Stephen. Don't let him go!" I yell.

He lets him go.

Down comes Jeffrey. He is on his back heading for the bottom pool, watching the sky race by. His father is splashing his way out of the middle pool. Instant replay.

"I said, don't ya run on the rocks!" screams the lifeguard. The paying public stops to watch. "Crazy guy," says the one in the fluorescent-green trunks.

I am fuming as I crash into the bottom pool. There he is, one foot underwater, his wide eyes watching as I frantically pull him out. "Jeffrey, are you okay?" He coughs twice and smiles as if to say, "What's all the fuss, Dad? Hey, it's the holidays!"

Some of us take longer than others to absorb the truth. In my case, it didn't sink in until we were huddled close together on my beach towel. As I hugged three wet little bodies close, I realized who I had set aside this vacation for. Sadly, it wasn't for them. Nor was it for their mom. Quite simply, I had engaged myself in the same behavior that is responsible for every single relational problem. For the breakup of every country. For every civil and not-so-civil war. It is this: selfishness.

"Lord Jesus," I pray, "I'm sorry."

Looking up, I see that my wonderful wife has returned, bearing ice cream and a knowing grin. "How did it go?"

"Not so good," I tell her. "But it's going to get better. I promise."

She begins to laugh. That's not hard for someone who enjoyed the whole spectacle from the safety of the ice-cream stand.

———

No one is so empty as when he is filled with himself.

14

The Wake-up Call

"WOW! FIRST A DRUM AND NOW CYMBALS! THANKS GRANDMA AND GRANDPA!"

66 ―――――――――――――――――――――――――

*Next week there can't be any crisis. My
schedule is already full.*

　　　　　　　　—Henry A. Kissinger

*A habit cannot be tossed out the window, it
must be coaxed down the stairs a step at a
time.*

　　　　　　　　—Mark Twain

*For all sad words of tongue or pen,
The saddest are these: "It might have been!"*

　　　　　　　　—John Greenleaf Whittier

*The journey of ten thousand miles begins with
a simple phone call.*

　　　　　　　　—Confucius Bell

―――――――――――――――――――― **99**

For 31 years he has been my father. I call him "Dad." His humor in tough times has been a wonder, his 50 years of faithfulness to my mother an inspiration.

It's not hard, though, to find fault in Dad. For one thing, he worries too much: about his health, about his wife, about his kids. We tease him, but we all know he can't help it. After all, worrying is hereditary. His father had it, and his father's grandchildren inherited it, too.

A plaque hangs above Dad and Mom's bed: "Thou wilt keep him in perfect peace, whose mind is stayed on Thee because he trusteth in Thee" (Isaiah 26:3). The words have hung there since I was born. Dad reads them often. Still he worries. And until recently, something else bothered me about Dad. If you have a minute, I'll tell you about it.

It's 8:30 P.M. The kids are in bed, and finally I'm able to turn the game on. The wrong team is winning and now the phone is ringing. I get it.

"Hello...hi, Dad...oh, I just sat down to watch the game....Ya, they're losing again...." My voice trails off as he begins to tell me about his day. He's going to see the doctor soon, and for Dad, *dentist* and *doctor* are synonyms.

Why now, Dad? I finally get a few minutes to take it easy and the phone rings. It's been a busy day. I was hoping to relax a little tonight. Can't you see I don't have time to talk?

The conversation continues, and then: "Well, you have yourself a good night, son."

"Thanks, Dad. Goodnight."

The next day begins early. I am swamped, you see. There is work to be done. Important work. The Lord's work. If I don't do it, it won't get done.

When evening arrives, I am tired out. And the phone rings.

"Hi, Dad....Yes, I'm just reading to the kids."

"Well, I won't keep you then."

But he does keep me. He's not feeling very well, he says. I'll come and see him—maybe—I say. But I don't. And again I ask myself the same questions: *Why now? Can't he tell I'm busy?*

In the morning I am back at it. Outside my office window snowflakes fall unnoticed, sirens sound, and there is a scurry of activity. An accident? A tragedy? I am too busy to care. After all, there are deadlines to meet, people to see, questions to ask. Once again I am comfortably entrenched at the center of my universe, all wrapped up in good intentions.

The phone rings.

"It's for you, Phil. It's your mom."

"Hi, Mom."

"Phil," her voice is wavering, "they've just taken Dad in the ambulance. I think it's a heart attack."

"Are you at home?"

"Yes," is all she can manage.

"I'll be right there."

Questions flood my mind during the five-minute run to their home. *Will I ever talk to him again? He doesn't phone that often; I should have known something was wrong. What if I would have...and what about Mom?*

On the way to the hospital, my mother is surprisingly calm. "It's true," she tells me, "God really does give us peace." I wish I could feel that peace. I have left too many things undone. Too many things unsaid. Oh, Lord, give me another chance.

We enter Dad's room. He is as white as the sheets, wired to various digital machines. Mom reaches down and begins to rub his hands.

We talk, we pray, and the doctor arrives. "It's not as serious as we thought," he says. Sitting in the corner of the room, I feel tears come as strangers to my eyes.

Dad, there are some things I need to say, before it's too late. You worry about your health and the future. And I have tritely told you that God will be there. But now I want to say that I will be there, too. Just as you were there to wipe my fevers away. Just as you left work early to watch me play hockey. As you took time for me, so I will for you. You can bank on it. As much as I am able, I will face this thing we call aging with you. For someone who loves me as much as you do, it's the least I can do.

A year has passed since that day.

And now, "Hello, Dad. We were wondering if you and Mom could join us for our annual World Series bash.... Okay... well, you know what to bring.... See you Wednesday."

On Wednesday my parents arrive. You should see them: Toronto Blue Jays hats on their heads, packages of baseball cards in their pockets. They are hardly acting their age. From the window three children greet their coming with excited squeals. What they don't know is that their grandparents have waited since baseball was invented for a Canadian team to reach the World Series. Now we will celebrate the best way possible—together.

Ignoring the advice of the Commission for the Containment of Cholesterol, we serve up hot dogs, peanuts, potato chips, and pop. This is one of a very few meals each year when Dad feels he can splurge. And it is the only meal when the television is allowed center stage. We sit with our hats on, cheering wildly, looking very much like fanatics. Perhaps there is no other description for those who love a sport that manages to cram three minutes of action into three hours.

And in the end the score does not matter because, long after I forget the outcome, I will remember that we were together. Long after I forget who hit that tenth-inning home run, I will remember that we enjoyed each other. That we laughed. That we talked. And that, while I had the chance, the right words were said. For this, Lord, I will be forever grateful.

———

We are judged by what we finish,
not by what we start.

15
Tithings of Joy

"OUR DONATIONS HAVE DOUBLED SINCE WE HAD THAT THING INSTALLED!"

66 ——————————————————————

There are three conversions necessary: the conversion of the heart, mind and the purse. Of the three it may well be that we moderns find the conversion of the purse the most difficult.
—Martin Luther

Having enough money is nowhere near as much fun as I thought it was going to be when I didn't have any.
—Andy Rooney

No one would remember the Good Samaritan if he only had good intentions. He had money as well.
—Margaret Thatcher

Make all you can, save all you can, and give all you can.
—John Wesley

—————————————————————— **99**

For those of you who are unfamiliar with the term or whose consciences need another none-too-subtle reminder, tithing is the act of giving a percentage of one's income to God.

It was always a complete joy for me as a child, this tithing. On Sundays my parents would entrust me with a small percentage of their percentage, which I would jingle in my pocket all the way to church before dropping it loudly into the offering plate.

But as I grew in stature and deviousness, my enthusiasm for the whole process dwindled somewhat. After all, I had learned the market value of those quarters.

ME: "Stan, look at this."

STAN: "Wow! Fifty cents! Where did you get that?"

ME: "From my mom."

STAN: "What's it for?"

ME: "Just so's we could spend it."

STAN: "Wow, your mom's cool!"

ME: "Ya. My mom's cool. Let's go blow it, eh?"

And we did. We *really* blew it. You see, in those days 50 cents became a lot of candy, and boys with sugar on the brain tend to forget that mothers always clean under their boys' beds.

MOM: "Philip, what is this?"
ME: "Uh, that's a lot of candy. May I have some?"
MOM: "I found it under your bed. Where did you get it?"
ME: "From Stan Kirk."
MOM: "Let's phone him then."
ME: "Um, well, no. Actually, you know that money you gave me for the offering?"
MOM: "Okay. Go get the strap, Philip."

Then at the tender age of 14, while working on a farm, my enthusiasm for the tithe was rekindled for good. After several hours in a dusty grain bin, I became gravely ill, which is to say I discovered cleaning granaries was not a vocation I wished to pursue. Convincing myself of nausea, I decided that upon the farmer's soon arrival I would inform him of my condition and he would compassionately rush me home where I could follow another calling.

The farmer, however, whose watch had evidently fallen down a deep, dark hole, did not soon arrive. I waited... and waited. Lunchtime came. My employer, I am sure, sat down to roast beef and the trimmings. I sat in a wheat field, wondering if he would ever arrive. To busy myself, I figured out how much I was making. These large figures led me, quite obviously, to the subject of tithing. I told God that I would once again begin to tithe 10 percent of my earnings if He would make the farmer come and get me.

The farmer did not come.

I told God I would tithe 11 percent if the farmer came VERY SOON AND HAD MY LUNCH IN HIS PICK-UP. This negotiating continued until the farmer found his watch and I lost a very healthy portion of my earnings. For life.

Wishing to save my children from such an experience and instill the value of giving at the same time, I recently brought home a little container. It is from a well-known mission and it says "vacuum-packed" on top, which—let's face it—is a physical impossibility because of the large slit that accommodates coins. A label on the side, however, makes clear the container's purpose: "Street Children Ministry. Help for needy children in developing countries."

I was excited about the idea. From time to time we would let the children insert loose change in the slot until the can was quite full of pennies, nickels, and dimes. I might even slip in the odd quarter, but I would withhold "loonies," our Canadian dollar coins, for my own private "loony collection."

"How does it work, Daddy?" Rachael asks after planting a welcome-home kiss on my ear.

"Well, this is where we'll put money to help some boys and girls who don't have as much as we do." Pulling some pennies and a nickel from my pocket, I hand them to her. "Here, put these in."

Soon all three kids are lined up. They insert the coins, then shake the container. Unlike the Coke machine, nothing comes out, but that does not deter their enthusiasm.

"What will the boys and girls use these for?" asks Stephen.

"Some missionaries will buy them food and clothes," I reply.

Weeks pass. To my delight, the can slowly fills. Instead of buying certain things, the kids learn to put change in the container. What better way to teach them a lesson it has taken me decades to learn? Ah, the joy of giving.

Then one day: "Honey, have you seen my loonies? I put them right here in the cupboard."

Ramona turns and looks at me with a grin. "Well, the kids found them," she says. "And you've done such a good job of telling them about those needy children..."

Ah, yes. The joy of giving.

―――――――

Many are willing to give God credit, few are willing to give Him cash.

16

Deinonychus and the Big Bang

66 ————————————————————————————

If evolution destroys anything, it does not destroy religion but rationalism.
                                    —G.K. Chesterton

I don't have the evidence to prove God doesn't exist, but I so strongly suspect He does not that I don't want to waste my time.
                                    —Isaac Asimov

Man prefers to believe what he prefers to be true.
                                    —Francis Bacon

I don't think we crawled out of the mud some place. I think we were created.
                                    —Mel Gibson

In the absence of any other proof, the thumb alone would convince me of God's existence.
                                    —Isaac Newton

———————————————————————————— **99**

I am not a strong proponent of the evolutionary theory. Oh sure, I have taken my children to the zoo, and I must admit there are definite similarities between the actions of certain of the species and the antics of certain of my offspring. But, you see, my wife and I have applied the cornerstone of this same ideology to our children's rooms, and it simply doesn't work.

Just this morning, for instance, Ramona shut the door on the very area where the Big Bang itself had occurred. Hours later, I opened it, hoping to see my son's room cleaned, the walls painted, perhaps some new furniture. But it was much the way he left it, and we did not have 360 million years to wait.

On the other hand, I don't have much trouble believing that large reptiles called dinosaurs roamed the earth many years ago. In fact, we have one in our house at this very moment. He is in the hallway, two claws on each front leg poised menacingly at his little brother.

"Stephen, what are you doing?" I ask.

"We're playing dinosaurs. I'm a deinonychus," he growls.

"What's Jeffrey?"

"He's a deinonychus, too." More growling.

"They don't eat each other, do they?"

"No, they just eat smaller dinosaurs. Like Rachael."

Our children's fixation with dinosaurs has come as no small shock to my mother. Since she was born with the same natural affection toward reptiles that bugs have to windshields, the following scene was played out often during my childhood.

> ME: "Mother, lookee here."
> MOM: "What is it, Philip?"
> ME: "Uh, I found it out back. It's a salamander."
> MOM: "Aaaaaaahhhhh!"
> DAD: "Son, would you please go and get the smelling salts?"

I have endeavored to keep this legacy for loathing lizards alive in our family, but it has been difficult to keep my own children from getting *into* dinosaurs.

It did not help when a neighbor child (who shall remain anonymous, although for the sake of this book we'll call him Joel McClanahan) discovered, after much excavation, that our "D" encyclopedia contained some hideous pictures. Joel should have closed the book. He should have asked us to tape the pages shut. Instead, he showed the hideous pictures to my son. Since then, we have sheltered and fed an iguanodon, a triceratops, but mostly a deinonychus.

Deinonychuses, according to the latest treasure trove of fun pictures my son brought home from the library, lived roughly 225 million years ago (before many of my high school teachers). The deinonychus had a big claw, shaped like a terrible sword. (I am telling you this so you will understand how frightening it is to encounter a live one 225 million years later in your very own hallway.)

My study of these huge reptiles has done little to endear me to them. For one thing, I can rarely spell their names, let alone pronounce them. But I am adjusting. I think. What I like best is tucking a gentle, plant-eating baby brontosaurus into bed.

"Daddy, you didn't read me a story." It is almost bedtime in the land of children and dinosaurs. Baby Brontosaurus sits on the couch.

"I know, Stephen. You get a book. I'll read it to you." So as not to disappoint me, he brings his library book and cuddles up beside me. It's called *All About Dinosaurs*.

Opening the book, I begin to read aloud: "Many scientists now feel sure that birds developed from dinosaurs. They say that the dinosaurs did not entirely die out. Instead, they became the robins, crows, eagles, and other birds we see today."

I look down at my son. His nose is wrinkled. He is wearing his *yeah-sure-right-Dad-you're-making-this-up-as-you-go* expression.

"Remember the robin we fed last summer? What was his name?" I ask.

"Gus-Gus."

"Do you think he might have been a little dinosaur a long time ago?"

"Ha!" he answers, his wrinkle turning to a grin.

"Stephen, people have to make up funny things when they pretend there's no God. Some of them say we came from mud and monkeys. What does the Bible say?"

"I don't know."

"In the beginning... what?"

"Um, God created the heavens and the earth."

"You're right." The Bible says that God made the birds, the fish, the animals. And it says that He made you and me, too. Aren't you glad we came from God, not monkeys?"

"Yep. Did God make dinosaurs?" he asks.

"Yes, but I don't know if they looked like the ones in this book."

"I like them," he says.

"And I like you, Stephen. Come with me. We have one more thing to do before I tuck you in." He takes my hand and off we go. A father and his baby brontosaurus. Off to clean up the Big Bang.

———

Do not enshrine ignorance just because
there is so much of it.

17
Coming Out on Top

"

When young, you adjust your hair to the existing hairstyle; when old, you adjust your hairstyle to the existing hair.

—K.P. Ramachandran

Let not thy thoughts run on what thou lackest, as much as on what thou already hast.

—Marcus Aurelius

Contentment is a pearl of great price, and whoever procures it at the expense of ten thousand desires makes a wise and a happy purchase.

—John Balguy

Youth and age touch only the surface of our lives.

—C.S. Lewis

"

I don't often purchase magazines at the check-out counter. But on this occasion, surrounded by frenzied shoppers, I couldn't help noticing (right next to Murphy Brown) the smiling faces of several of the most successful movie stars in cinematic history. What really interested me was not their faces but the fact that they were having a similar problem to mine. If I paid the cover price (only $2.95), they would tell me how to fix it.

I first became aware of The Problem while brushing my teeth one night. My wife, who would never say anything to intentionally hurt anyone (even me) was also brushing hers and standing over me while I rinsed. When I stood up I could tell by the look on her face that she had seen something important. "YOORGOOBLLLD!" she said through a mouthful of toothpaste. After rinsing, she repeated five words that have haunted me ever since: "You are going bald, Phil."

Now this came as no surprise. We have mirrors around the home and I am reminded of the aging process when my wife and I meet people. "Nice to meet you, Phil. And what did you say was your granddaughter's name?" But my "granddaughter" had never actually verbalized the startling truth before: "You are going bald, Phil."

"I know," I said, before flicking my toothbrush at her.

Hoping to curb the problem, I had already conducted research which had taught me the following.

1. *Don't comb it differently.* My own father—who went bald back when the earth was flat—did this. The trick here is to grow your hair very long on one side and comb it carefully over the deceased area. This does not work. This does not even fool small children, who have been known to point out this fact during church. "HEY, MOMMY. I JUST SAW THE BOTTOM OF MR. WILSON'S HEAD." I have also heard it suggested that you grow your eyebrows to their full length and comb them back. I have yet to see this done effectively.

2. *Don't use Minoxidil.* Researchers tell us that Minoxidil is the only proven hair-growing drug. "Here, Mr. Callaway. This works on an eight-ball; it should work on you," they say, opening their cash registers. What these same researchers will not tell us is that Minoxidil *has been largely ineffective in men.* This is true. And what they will *definitely* not tell men is that it works for women, whom other researchers have conclusively proven do not need it.

3. *Don't consider relocation.* The basic principle here is simply redistribution: taking hair from an area where it exists and moving it to the dead zone. This is something you will not want to try at home, but skilled surgeons will be happy to insert individual hairs into pinholes made with hypodermic needles. Unfortunately, these little operations will end up costing you about $10,000 and might even require years of treatment and even more cash, should the hair surrounding the transplant choose to fall out.

4. *Consider classical music.* After extensive research, Daiichi Pharmaceutical, a leading Japanese drug producer, is promoting a compact disc of Mozart's music (now available only in pharmacies). The company claims that the music will soothe the listener, relieve stress, and even reverse the balding process. They may be on to something

there, although I have conducted similar research on my father in which I play Petra compact discs for him. This causes his head to *appear* hairier.

Standing in line with Murphy Brown that day, I reconsidered these four facts, then did what most men who are living under a recession would do: I reached for my wallet and pulled out an extra $2.95.

Upon arriving home, I excitedly turned to page 98, seeking some timely advice. There they were: Bill Murray, Jack Nicholson, Bruce Willis, Ted Danson, Ron Howard, and several others, each of them hiding their baldness behind— you guessed it—a baseball cap. *Hey,* I thought, *so this is the secret? Keep it under your hat?* I was so disappointed that I decided then and there to make a little list of my own.

Here it is, men:

1. *Use your head for something else.* Tony Campolo has pointed out (pun intended) that there are better uses for hormones than growing hair. Concern yourself with what's inside your head, not what's on top.

2. *Be content with such hair as you have.* In a society that spends billions of dollars researching ways to postpone the inevitable, it's easy to miss what is really important. Second Corinthians 4:16 says, "Though outwardly we are wasting away, yet inwardly we are being renewed day by day." As I grow older, I trust my wife will enjoy my company more because I am content with who God has made me. Content because of what He has given me. Content because of what He is doing inside my head.

So, men, I hope you've benefited from this advice. Should it fail, there are always a few things you can fall back on. You could keep a hat nearby and—oh, yes—you could brush your teeth alone.

———

Much of what we see depends on what we are looking for.

18

The Return of September

66 ———————————————————————————

That energy which makes a child hard to manage is the energy which afterward makes him a manager of life.

— Henry Ward Beecher

I believe that children reared in homes where morality is taught and lived rarely become delinquents.

— J. Edgar Hoover

Prayer requires more of the heart than of the tongue.

— Adam Clarke

Seven days without prayer makes one weak.

— Allen E. Bartlett

——————————————————————— **99**

At the risk of shattering my mother's firm belief that during my elementary school days I was not only a founding member of The Society for the Education of the Three Wise Men, but also Saint Francis of Assisi's mentor, I relate the following true story.

I was in grade five and I was frightened. Very frightened. Before me was a teacher whose presence struck immeasurable fear into my ten-year-old heart.

"And what," she asked in a voice that would have sent Napoleon scurrying from Italy, "is the punishment for being kicked out of music class three times, Philip?" My name she tossed out much like one would a day-old tuna casserole.

Unable to force the word through my quivering lips, I picked up a pencil and wrote "s-t-r-a-p" in very small letters It was while handing the paper to her that I realized I was closing in on some kind of record. This would be my third sampling of the dread leather. In one year the rod of correction had graced my seat of understanding more times than all my siblings put together.

If there was an up side to the whole experience, it was the celebrity status that accompanied such events. Classmates would line the halls to ask what it felt like. "Did you cry?" was the most common question.

"Naw," was the most common lie. For some reason no one ever asked, "Well then, while you were in there did you happen to see who was doing all that yelling?"

Instead they would ask, "What did you get it for?"

"I put a pin in Stan Kirk," I replied on this occasion.

"Wow," they would say and I would strut down the hall, leaving them standing in small circles of respectful conversation.

"You know," I said, walking home later with Steve Porr, thankful I was not riding a bike, "I think it's the pants."

He stopped throwing dirt clods and looked at me. "The pants?".

"Yes, the pants. Every time I get sent to the office I look down and I have these same green pants on."

"She doesn't like your pants?"

"No, I don't think that's it."

"Well, where did you get them?" he asked, looking at my pants.

"That's not the point," I said. "The point is we've got to do something about these pants."

"Like what? Burn them?"

"That's the most ridiculous idea!" I replied with wisdom beyond my years. Then on second thought I said, "Sure, let's burn 'em."

And so it was that we found ourselves in the glow of a bonfire that June afternoon. And—believe it or not—we burned my green cotton pants.

"Do you suppose a little demon might run out?" Steve asked, ever eager to discuss the supernatural.

"I don't know. Let's watch," I replied. And we did.

That was 25 years ago now, and I am just as scared today as the day I faced the s-t-r-a-p. You see, I have kids of my own, and September is coming. I also know "by heart" a lot of Scripture verses including the one about the sins of the fathers visiting the children.

So as I weigh these thoughts, I find myself asking the same question that Galileo and like-minded individuals undoubtedly pondered throughout written history: Is there any hope at all for my offspring?

The obvious answer is no. Anyone who superstitiously burned his pants in grade five is bound to have serious problems raising kids. And I find little comfort in the words of those who would prescribe only the latest child-rearing techniques.

The answer, I believe, is found in the lives of parents like mine, who have talked more about me on their knees than anywhere else. For apart from God's grace and the prayers of my parents, I would be walking the same wide path that too many of my friends are. We all must choose. But I will continue to pray every day that the same God who loved a mischievous little troublemaker enough to turn his life around will do as much for his children.

My wife is in full agreement. She just returned from a shopping spree and has managed to snag a great little outfit for our six-year-old's first day of school. It's a white pullover with the number 32 on the front, and—would you believe it?—a pair of green cotton pants.

———

There seems to be a cure these days for everything but heredity.

Kids in the Kingdom

THE 90'S DAD: ABLE TO SPEND TIME WITH HIS KIDS WHILE STILL INDULGING IN HIS FAVORITE SPORT.

66 ———————————————————————————

When I played pro football, I never set out to hurt anybody deliberately . . . unless it was, you know, like a league game or something.
—Dick Butkus

I've got three children now. Things that I felt were extremely important before, now are totally irrelevant. You have to realign your values.
—Rod Stewart

The Christian home is the Master's workshop where the processes of character molding are silently, lovingly, faithfully and successfully carried on.
—Richard Monckton
Milnes

The way to be saved is not to delay, but to come and take.
—Dwight L. Moody

——————————————————————— **99**

For much of my life my priorities were somewhat suspect. For instance, golf followed baseball, which followed hockey, which followed absolutely nothing. Like many other Canadian boys, I ate and slept sports. In November, my brothers and I would lace up our ice skates and leave them on until Mother pried them off sometime in late March. Long summer days were spent chasing anything that could be kicked, rolled, slid, or bounced. In the evenings we conducted phone-in sports talk shows and entertained dreams of future stardom.

Of course, children have a way of helping us rearrange those priorities. It started for me in the most unlikely place: the golf course.

Tightly gripping my trusty three-wood, I addressed the ball. Before me lay the neatly groomed greenery of the first hole. Behind me stood my son. Today I would teach him everything there was to know about a game I had come to love. Since golf is better caught than taught, I would demonstrate. He, I hoped, would catch.

I was confident. Poised. Certain.

"Watch, Stephen," I said.

Firmly planting my feet, I brought the club back and in one smooth, practiced motion sliced a brand-new Top Flite into the muddiest creek this side of the Euphrates. I was not a happy golfer.

"Did it go into the water?"

"Yes, Stephen."

"Is that how you do it?"

"Well, uh, not exactly. I'll try again."

Several holes and many balls later I began to realize I was going about this all wrong. *If he is to acquire a love for sports,* I thought, *perhaps he should watch someone who knows what they're doing.*

And so it was, a few days later, that we found ourselves in the middle of several thousand baseball fans searching for a glimmer of hope in a 9-1 thrashing of the home team.

"See, Stephen, there's the pitcher. He's looking at the catcher, and the catcher's going to wiggle his fingers."

"Huh?"

"He's telling the pitcher what kind of pitch to throw. You watch now."

My son is watching all right. He is watching the man with a huge box on his head move slowly toward us, his megaphone voice stuck on, "*Get your popcorn, peanuts, candies, beer....*"

"Daddy, what's beer?"

Oh, boy. "Uh, well, son beer is..." His attention is diverted to the mascot. The catlike creature is coming our way, surrounded by dozens of kids hoping for a hug. Stephen shrinks into the seat beside me. "I don't like him," he says. But he does like the food. And so we consume popcorn, peanuts, and some orange pop. As the score reaches 11-1, we head for the exit.

It has been a big day for a little boy, but as we point our Ford homeward he has yet to run out of questions. The conversation moves from ice cream to beer, from baseball to lions—and finally to Jesus.

His questions astound me at times, especially since a friend of his was killed in a car accident. "If Janella is in heaven," he asks, "does she have nail scars in her hands?" and, "If good guys go to heaven, where do bad guys go?"

"Remember the verse we've been saying at bedtime? 'For God so loved the world that he gave his one and only Son, that whoever believes in him shall not perish but have eternal life'?" Stephen finishes the verse with me. "Well, when we believe that Jesus died for our sins, He writes our names down in His book and we will go to live with Him when we die."

"But where do bad guys go?" Stephen rarely listens this carefully.

"Another verse in the Bible says that those who don't have their names in God's book will go to a place called hell."

"What will hell be like?"

"Well, it will be a sad place because Jesus won't be there."

"I don't want to go there."

"You can be sure you don't go there."

"How?"

"You can tell Jesus that you're sorry for the bad things you've done. And that you're glad He died for your sins. And you can ask Him to come into your heart."

"Okay. You help me."

By the time we finish praying, my heart is soaring.

"Play Scott Wesley Brown, Daddy."

I reach for the tape deck.

"Glory, hallelujah, look what God is doing," comes through loud and clear. Stephen taps his feet, and a tear finds its way down my cheek. This is one of those moments that parents never forget. A moment that parents pray for. A moment that causes angels to party and names to be written down. Signed in blood. Forever.

I can hear some of you saying that Stephen is too young, that a four-year-old can't know enough to make an eternal decision. Perhaps you are right. But I believe he will renew that commitment as he understands more about it. And for now I am thankful he has obeyed a voice that still beckons to all of us: "Unless you change and become like little children, you will never enter the kingdom of heaven."

"Daddy, will we play baseball in heaven?" Stephen's favorite song has finished, but not his questions.

"Would you like that?"

"Yeah."

"Well, I learned something today, Stephen. I learned that there are things much better than baseball. You see, baseball only goes nine innings, and somebody always loses. Heaven will last forever, and you only win there."

"I like that," he says.

"Me, too."

———

*Child-rearing is really
heir-conditioning.*

"

The value of marriage is not that adults produce children, but that children produce adults.

—Peter de Vries

God can't use unscarred vessels.

—Charles R. Swindoll

All men desire peace, but very few desire those things that make for peace.

—Thomas à Kempis

"

I suppose It all began in grade two when Miss Barzley came to town. Before Miss Barzley, I didn't know how to spell *terror*. But after that first visit, the very sight of her white Health Department Cruiser was enough to send our entire class into frenzied seclusion.

"I just saw The Car," would whisper Leslie Kolibaba, horror etched on his seven-year-old face. And we would tremble in anticipation.

Now you must understand that the first time Miss Barzley came to town, we trusted her entirely. And so, like very young lambs, we were lined up single file in a darkened hallway.

I remember standing near the back of the line, unsure of the results of reaching the front. Those who had gone on ahead were returning with "attempted amputation" written all over their voices. "Oooowwww," was how they put it. And they were rolling down their sleeves. Oh, how I longed for the hand of my father. He would show Miss Barzley!

But each of us entered The Room alone, where sat the health nurse.

She was a rather imposing figure, even without the large needle in her hand, but its presence prevented us from seeing our reward for good behavior: the sugar cubes.

"Roll up your sleeve. It won't hurt," lied Miss Barzley, who was clearly hardened beyond hope. Then she poked us. It took just a moment, but we were scarred for life.

———————

Twenty-three years later, when my wife informed me that the time had arrived for our son, Stephen, to receive the shot some adult members of our civilized society have decided to give all five-year-olds, I volunteered to take him to the nurse. I was, after all, the obvious choice to comfort him. Having been poked myself, I knew what he was facing. I would hold his hand. Besides, brave fathers living in the nineties do these things.

"Will it hurt, Daddy?" We were on our way to the clinic, and I had just informed my son of the reason. The tears came quickly as the news shattered his gentle world of cowboy games and toy guns.

"Well, son," I remembered an old lie told me by a young dentist, "it will pinch a little."

"But what will they do?"

"They will put the needle into your arm and it will come out at your knee."

"Naw," he laughed and began to wipe his tears, knowing that anything his father could joke about couldn't be too serious.

"If you are brave, we'll go out for a treat after."

It was enough, for the moment. But upon our arrival, events took a turn for the worse. Unlike my hallway experience, our surroundings were pleasant and the nurse was not imposing. But the needle was much the same shape and Stephen was terrified.

Incentives to bravery were offered him: not sugar cubes, but pencils that smell nice (as if children need another reason to chew them), stickers, a coloring book, more stickers, no-charge checking, a registered retirement savings plan—anything. JUST RELAX, PLEASE! But he wouldn't relax, and at last I held my horrified son tight as the nurse delivered the goods.

One month has passed. The pain has subsided, but not the memory. Today we are on our way to another clinic. We will have our warts removed. Together. It seems fear is not the only thing he has inherited.

"What will they do?" asks Stephen.

"They will probably have to take our feet off to work on the warts," answers his dad.

"Naw," he laughs.

"I'll be there. Remember, I've got a wart, too. And if we are real brave," I say, "we will get a treat after."

At the clinic, Stephen is terrified again. My presence brings little comfort, my words even less. After all, I was of little help during the last encounter. Why should this be any different?

In the doctor's office we wait. The seasons come and go. Finally the doctor arrives with a bubbling vat of something.

"It's liquid nitrogen," says the doc. "Minus 300 degrees."

Oh good, he's going to freeze our feet off.

"You go first, Phil."

"Uh, me? Um, okay, doctor."

Slowly I remove my sock. He dips a long Q-tip into the vat and rubs it on my wart. A little boy watches nervously, his eyes darting between my false smile and my afflicted foot. "See, son, it's going to be okay."

When Stephen's turn arrives, he is relatively calm. After all, he reasons, if Daddy can handle it, so can I.

Minutes later, we are seated in a nearby restaurant. Our feet are a little tender, but our spirits are good. It is time for our above-and-beyond-the-call-of-bravery awards. When they arrive, a little boy has some questions.

"Will our warts stay gone?"

"I think so."

"Did yours hurt?"

"A little bit."

"Mine hurt. But you were there."

Then I tell him of Miss Barzley, of needles, of waiting in a darkened hallway to get poked. "I always wished my daddy was there with me, Stephen."

Stephen has run out of ice cream and is eyeing the pop machine.

"Are you glad Daddy was there today?" I ask him.

"Yep. But even more," he says, "I'm glad you got poked."

———

A door opened today. And I saw God in the words of my son. Because, you see, as much as I have marveled at the reality of Christ's presence, as much as I have been comforted by His reassuring words, never before had I realized exactly why His suffering means so much to me. As Isaiah put it, "He was pierced for our transgressions, he was crushed for our iniquities; the punishment that brought us peace was upon him, and by his wounds we are healed" (Isaiah 53:5).

Perhaps Stephen would say, "I'm glad He was poked."

Me too. And because He was wounded, nothing will haunt us that He has not handled. Because He was bruised, we can look an uncertain future in the face. Because He was pierced, we have peace.

Whether you're standing in a hospital ward, an empty house, or at the back of the line in a long, dark hallway, that's good news.

═══

God never takes us where He has not been.

66 ───────────────────────────────────────

Money won't buy happiness, but it will pay the salaries of a huge research staff to study the problem.
                    —Bill Vaughan

I can think of nothing less pleasurable than a life devoted to pleasure.
                    —John D. Rockefeller, Jr.

Prosperity knits a man to the World. He feels that he is "finding his place in it," while really it is finding its place in him.
                    —C.S. Lewis

───────────────────────────────────── **99**

On those rare Sunday afternoons when I manage to remain awake, I have discovered a wealth of opportunity for family togetherness. Take this afternoon, for instance.

My son and I are sprawled out together on the couch where I am reading aloud from C.S. Lewis' *The Chronicles of Narnia*. He is clearly lapping up each word, intently studying my every inflection, my subtle vocal nuances the obvious key to his fascination.

Ah, quality time.

"Daddy," my blond son takes time out from his lapping—likely a question concerning the narrative. "Daddy, you're getting old."

"Um, why do you say that, Stephen?" I am calm, cool—sweating.

"You kinda look like Grandpa." My son's blue eyes are scrutinizing my countenance. My son. The one I have loved, sheltered, and clothed for more than five years. I will think of some fitting form of punishment for him now. I shall send him to his room until he is 21. Yes, I will feed him through the keyhole. After all, Mark Twain was right. This method solves other problems too: grocery bills, allowance, dating.

"What do you mean, I look like Grandpa?" The conversation has taken on an uncomfortably personal tone.

"You have lines on your head."

"No I don't... do I?"

"Yep."

"Where?"

"Here. Here and here. You're getting old."

Oh boy, I didn't need this today. I just blew out 30 candles, or at least most of them.

"Do you think I'm going to die soon, Stephen?"

"I don't know. How many are you?"

"I'm 30 years old."

"How many is that?"

"Well, it's this many, three times," I say, holding my hands up, all fingers outstretched. His blue eyes are bigger now. "Is that old, Stephen?"

"Yep, that's old."

Now, I realize it doesn't take a nuclear physicist to determine that my head is looking more like a mosquito-landing zone than the last ten seconds of a Grecian Formula commercial. But until now I thought I was doing all right. After all, 40 is old, but 30? No way.

Tonight I sit alone at the kitchen table. It's taken a while, but the truth is beginning to sink in: I am 30, no longer a kid. No longer do I watch "the big guys" play football on TV. I *am* "the big guys." No longer do the neighborhood children call me *Phil*. To them I am *Mr. Callaway*.

But what do I have to show for 30 years on planet Earth? Incredible wealth?

We have a car that's paid for. A guitar. A stereo that often works. But the house is a rental. And the cabin on the beach? Well, I drove by one once. No, three decades have not been kind to my wallet.

Fame?

Well, I saw Clint Eastwood once—on TV. And I have a close friend who sat on a plane near... You get the idea.

Getting up from the table, I head down the hall to perform my nightly ritual of checking on the kids. Jeffrey is sleeping. One leg hangs out of his crib, the other is crushing his stuffed dog. I quietly rearrange his legs and cover him.

Rachael is awake, reading to Mary, her favorite doll. I tuck her in for the third time. "Goodnight, Rachael."

From Stephen's room Twila Paris sings, "Fix your eyes on Jesus..." but Stephen's eyes are shut. Turning off his tape, I sit down on the bed. He stirs and rolls over.

My son, what shall I leave you? Wealth? Not if wealth is measured in things you can touch. Happiness? Not if happiness is the absence of problems. But if wealth can't be found in a loving family, I don't know where to look. And as sure as happiness, peace, and satisfaction are worth searching for, I have found them through faith in Jesus Christ.

Yes, my son, we *are* rich: rich in relationships, rich in memories, rich in fun. It may not look that good in the will, but when you're approaching retirement at the speed of light, it's worth smiling about.

We are rich in proportion to the amount of
things we do not want.

Some Final Thoughts

It's getting late. The sun has gone to bed. So has my wife. The children, too. All, that is, except Rachael. Tonight, as I attempt to put the finishing touches on this book, she has brought her pillow to my study door. Insomniacs Anonymous is about to convene.

The past few months have been like this. "When are you gonna put those games back on the computer?" the children ask as I struggle for the last line in an important paragraph. Or, "Come, I wanna show you someping." And so I go to see "someping" and my paragraph remains unfinished.

What do you do with children like that?

Well, tonight I lay a soft blanket on the floor beside me, hold Rachael for a few minutes, then tuck her in. She is now conversing quietly with Kermit, a 49-cent plastic toy.

It's been quite a week, this one. When a father attempts to become an author, his children never let him forget that he is first a father.

On Tuesday we rented a children's video. I don't remember the title, but I can't forget the opening scene. Sitting on a blanket, trying to juggle popcorn, juice, and three children, we watched the screen as the young heroine marched angrily into her room and cut her hair off. After this the movie became quite enjoyable, but I wondered why Rachael wasn't interested in it (normally we have to pry her off the television set with large steel instruments). While the rest of us watched the screen, she went out to the kitchen where we could hear her sweet voice singing softly. I had no reason to believe she was doing anything else.

Moments later she returned with a sheepish grin on her face and a pair of scissors in her hand. I say "sheepish" because she had just sheared her own wool. Were it not for an unavoidable urge to laugh, I suppose I would have cried. Ah, how I loved that hair! Now her mother had to trim it short and dump the long, blonde curls unceremoniously into the garbage.

"Rachael, don't you ever do that again!"

"I won't, Mommy."

On Thursday, our six-year-old son stood before me with a big grin on his face. Combining his sister's example, the best of intentions, and a good pair of scissors, he had treated himself to a reverse mohawk.

After the laughter died down, I got to thinking about those events. About the influence that a TV show can have on a child. About the impact of friends. Of peers. Of teachers. Of politicians. Of those who don't always have our children's best interests in mind.

Outside my open window all is quiet. In this rural setting we are spoiled by peacefulness. The only sounds at this hour are the occasional cricket and the click of my computer keyboard. Quietness... stillness... peace.

But I am not naive enough to think that the quietness will last. We live in a world where, for now, wrong seems to overpower right, where evil men and women literally sell their souls to buy the hearts, the minds, the bodies of our children.

How about you? Do you ever wonder what kind of grown-ups today's children will become after viewing thousands of acts of violence and adultery before they are old enough to clean their rooms? Do you ever wonder what kind of parents they will make when their only role models cared just enough to shed a tear as they walked out? Do you ever wonder how children can make eternal decisions surrounded by people who can't see beyond the moment? Let's face it, these can be frightening days for parents.

But they don't need to be.

Tonight I kneel beside my chair, right here in the study. Unfortunately, it usually takes thoughts like these to bring me to this position. "Oh, Lord, please give Ramona and me wisdom to write Your Word on our children's hearts. To show them Your love. To teach them discernment while they are still young. And, Lord, thank You for all You are going to do."

Tonight, my friend, I pray the same for you. Whether you're old or young, whether you have children or not, I pray that this book has given you a small glimpse of how much our heavenly Father loves you. I pray you will know that because of His Son, Jesus Christ, we can stand with our families on the edge of the unknown with little to fear and everything to hope for.

And now, I really must go. You see, a little girl sleeps beside me and a Canadian winter is on the way. Getting up, I close the window and pick up Rachael. I wouldn't want her to catch a head cold. After all, this little lamb doesn't have quite as much wool as she did on Tuesday.

If you would like to send the author your comments or interesting accounts of life in your home, write:

Phil Callaway
P.O. Box 4576
Three Hills
Alberta, Canada
T0M 2A0